The DeWire Guide
to
Lighthouses of the Pacific Coast

CALIFORNIA, OREGON, AND WASHINGTON

by

Elinor DeWire

PARADISE CAY PUBLICATIONS, INC.

ARCATA, CA

Printed in China.
First Edition, Expanded and Revised.
ISBN 978-0-939837-86-1

Published by Paradise Cay Publications, Inc.
P. O. Box 29
Arcata, CA 95518-0029
800-736-4509
707-822-9163 Fax
paracay@humboldt1.com

Picture Credits

Bob Trapani 55

Bruce Robie 29, 44, 51, 65 (top), 67 (bottom), 68, 71 (bottom), 91 (bottom), 98, 131, 164, 166 (top), 168, 171 (top)

Chad Kaiser 137 (bottom)

Coast Guard Archives XIV, XVI, 10, 16, 18, 21 (bottom), 26, 35, 36, 48, 49 (top), 59 (bottom), 64, 65 (bottom), 69, 70, 71 (top), 77, 89, 92, 94, 110, 111, 112, 121, 127, 130, 157 (top), 158, 163, 165, 167, 174, 175 (top)

Coast Guard Museum Northwest 37, 53, 58, 84, 87, 101 (bottom), 106, 108, 109, 113, 114, 122, 148

Denise Wilks, Orcas Island Eclipse Charters 173

Derith Bennett 12, 17 (bottom),

Diane Gardetto 40

Doug Bingham 90

Gene Miller 38

Irving Conklin Collection, Nautical Research Center 73, 79, 107

Island County Historical Society 120, 160

Jerry & Nadine Tugel 39

Jessica DeWire 103 (bottom)

Jim Claflin X, 141-143

Jim Gibbs 99, 103 (top), 155 (top), 169

Jonathan DeWire 154, 182

Library of Congress XIII (top)

Linda Hudson 175 (bottom)

Lois Melville 137 (top)

Monterey Museum 25

National Archives 83

National Oceanic & Atmospheric Administration 93

National Park Service 45, 135

Nautical Research Center 23 (top), 41, 67 (top)

Points Northeast Historical Society 144

Santa Cruz City Museum 26 (top)

U.S. Lighthouse Society XII, 3, 43, 57, 58, 59 (bottom), 61, 74

Washington Lightkeepers Association 118, 119, 155

All other images are credited to the author or are from her collection.

To Derith Bennett,
Linda Terrell,
and Sharon Todd,

honorable members of the
"Ya, Ya Lighthouse Sisterhood,"
who frequently drag me along
on their Pacific Coast travels.

Table of Contents

Acknowledgments

No effort such as this ever comes together without help. I am grateful to the following groups and individuals for their encouragement and assistance:

The U.S. Coast Guard, Jeff Gales and the U.S. Lighthouse Society, Tim Harrison and the American Lighthouse Foundation, Colin MacKenzie and the Nautical Research Center, the National Archives, Dr. Robert Browning and the staff of the U.S. Coast Guard Archives, Capt. Gene Davis and the Coast Guard Museum Northwest, Washington Lightkeepers Association, Kraig Anderson and www.lighthousefriends.com, Bruce Robie, Derith Bennett, Carole Adams, Jeremy D'Entremont, Sandy Clunies, Candace Clifford, Barb Lyter, Gloria Wahlin, Janet Garcia, Chad Kaiser, Jim Gibbs, "The Lighthouse People, " and the many descendents of U.S. Lighthouse Establishment lightkeepers and Coast Guard lightkeepers who provided pictures and stories.

Thanks also to Jim Morehouse and the crew of Paradise Cay Publications for their interest in my work and diligent effort bringing this book into print.

As always, I treasure the encouragement and support of my family—husband Jon, daughter Jessica, son Scott, daughter-in-law Rebecca, and even little Elena Eloise, who may someday come to love lighthouses as much as her grandmother does.

Introduction

Lighthouses beguile us with their beauty and romance, their history and lore. During the night, their powerful beams reassure us, banishing the darkness and giving guidance to those who travel uncertain seas. By day, we delight in their marine surroundings and whimsical daymarks of bright colors and bold stripes. It's no wonder poets, painters, and photographers seek inspiration from lighthouses and tourists flock to their doors.

Wayne Wheeler, founder of the Washington-based U.S. Lighthouse Society sums it up well: "Everybody loves lighthouses!" Wheeler sees lighthouses as the quintessential emblems of civility. They offer both a welcome and a warning, and are revered by all for their humanitarian mission. The nonprofit society Wheeler helped charter in 1985 is among hundreds around the nation that endeavor to preserve lighthouses and educate the public about their history and national importance.

Lighthouse preservation is no small mission. In 1915, during the halcyon days of the U.S. Lighthouse Establishment, more than 1,000 lighthouses stood watch along our nation's shores. Today, about 675 remain. Some have fallen to the ravages of weather and time, but most are victims of changing technology. Modern forms of navigation using the invisible and silent signals of satellites have lessened the need for lighthouses. The few that remain on duty may someday become altogether obsolete.

Gone as well is the colorful era of the American lighthouse keeper, which can be traced back to 1716 when a colonial beacon went into service in Boston Harbor and a local man named George Worthylake was hired by the Massachusetts Bay Colony to tend the lighthouse. Candles produced that first feeble light. The tapers eventually gave way to oil and kerosene lamps, then gas burners, and eventually electricity. There were myriad contraptions to foil the fog too—cannons, bells, whistles, sirens, horns. The vigilant lighthouse keeper made sure the warnings sounded whenever the air became murky. During World War I, when lighthouse engineers began experimenting with robotic gadgets, the end of a vibrant era was in sight. Light and sound sensors could do the work of human hands, and they soon began to displace lightkeepers.

In 1939 the U.S. Coast Guard assumed control of the nation's lighthouses. The pace of automation accelerated. Lighthouses were costly to staff and the Coast Guard needed personnel to fill other positions. By the 1960s the push to make lighthouses self-sufficient had become a full-time effort. Under LAMP (Lighthouse Automation and Modernization Program), the Coast Guard evaluated lighthouses one by one, deciding to either discontinue them or automate them. In the early 1990s the last of the American lighthouse keepers retired when Boston Light was de-staffed and handed over the National Park Service. Lights were switched to automatic operations and padlocks were placed on tower doors.

The immediate result was a visible compromise of historic integrity. Windows and doors were boarded up, and old classical lenses gave way to plastic optics and solar panels. Eventually the dwellings and towers began to deteriorate or they fell victim to rampant vandalism. Public outcry at the loss of these treasured landmarks produced a groundswell of interest in saving them.

Many lighthouses were added to state and national registers of historic places. Nonprofit groups formed to adopt and care for them. Two large national organizations—the U.S. Lighthouse Society and the American Lighthouse Foundation—took the lead in the preservation effort by spearheading legislation to assure all old lighthouses would be saved. The outcome was the National Historic Lighthouse Preservation Act of 2002. The act transfers ownership of excess Coast Guard lighthouses to worthy private groups and government agencies.

Lighthouses are once again experiencing a heyday. In the past few decades, hundreds of them have been saved from vandalism and the wrecking ball to become museums or focal points of parks and recreation areas. A new kind of lightkeeper has emerged, one who doubles as a museum docent and park ranger, or a dedicated volunteer eager to share knowledge and open the door for visitors. The rescue of our historic sentinels is a symbolic reversal of mission: lighthouses were built to save people; now people are saving lighthouses.

This guidebook, now in a second, expanded edition, is a roundup of the existing lighthouses along the Pacific Coast of the United States—lighthouses in California, Oregon, and Washington. Most West Coast sentinels still exhibit a beacon each night, while a few serve only as daymarks. Many are favorite destinations for travelers. Their images appear on city seals, business logos, tourist brochures, media advertisements, and a plethora of souvenirs available in gift shops.

In the pages ahead are maps and brief histories of lighthouse development in each state. Existing individual lighthouses are profiled by state in a south-to-north geographic listing, including details such as nearest town, historical facts of interest, directions for finding the lighthouse, and contacts for further information. Here and there I've sprinkled a few interesting sidebars to provide glimpses into the deeper story of lighthouses. I hope these snapshots of history, along with the individual lighthouse entries, will encourage you to travel to the sentinels of the Pacific Coast. For more information about lighthouses of the Pacific Coast, refer to the list of online sources and books at the back of this guide.

It's important to note that modern skeleton towers and pole lights are not included in this guide. There is considerable debate as to what defines a lighthouse, and I will avoid that discussion here. Instead, I have chosen to include only what might be called "traditional lighthouses," or those the public would agree are visually attractive and historically significant. These are the wood, masonry, and metal-plate towers, often conical or cottage-style in form and with a significant architectural history. A few skeleton-type towers and ultra-modern lighthouses have been included, due to their historical significance.

As you visit lighthouses on the West Coast, remember to obey no-trespassing signs and to respect private property. Take only pictures, memories, and souvenirs for sale. To add to your enjoyment, you might consider keeping a journal of your lighthouse travels or purchasing a "Lighthouse Passport" from the U.S. Lighthouse Society to record the sites you visit. You also can track your travels online and swap news and comments with other lighthouse buffs at the U.S. Lighthouse Society's "Lighthouse Enthusiasts Community" at www.uslhs.org/resources_community.php.

Happy lighthouse hunting!

Elinor DeWire
Seabeck, Washington
2010

A Star to Steer By

If a lighthouse could be said to possess a soul, it would be the great light pouring from its lantern each night to guide home the lonely mariner. Like a star, it shines dependably and regularly every night. It can beam steadily or it can flash. Its beacon can be white, red to mark a danger area, or red and green to show the port and starboard sides of a channel. Clouds and fog may obscure the beam, but when the skies are clear a lighthouse is a bright star by which to steer.

What makes the great beacon in a lighthouse shine so brightly?

Over the centuries a variety of illuminants and light fixtures have been used in lighthouses. The earliest beacons were wood or coal braziers set atop piles of rock. Candelabras with dozens of tapers were hung in the first American lighthouses, followed by pan lamps and spider lamps with many oil wells and wicks. Light-keepers trimmed the wicks frequently to help them burn clean and clear, thus earning the nickname "wickies."

Large individual oil lamps came into use around 1800. These were placed in front of silvered reflectors to intensify their light. Circular wicks helped channel air for a more efficient flame. Later, small lenses were positioned in front of the lamps to further strengthen the light. Whale oil and fish oil were popular fuels, but lard oil and colza oil (made from turnip-like plants) also were used.

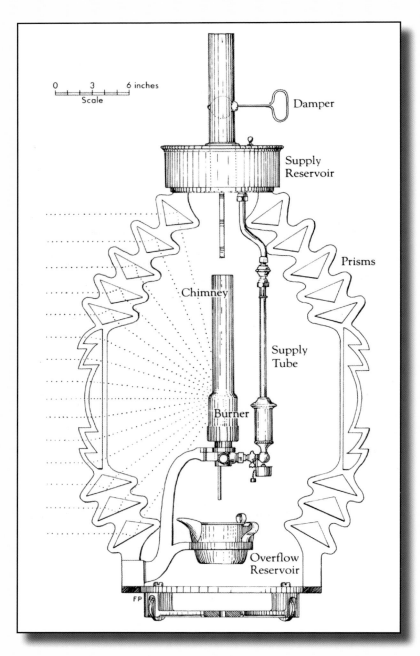

Lard Oil Lamp Inside a Small Fresnel Lens

Until the 1820s all lights were white and fixed, and they seldom could be seen more than a few miles away. There was no technology to make them flash. This changed when French physicist Augustin-Jean Fresnel developed a revolutionary lenticular system. He placed mirrors and prisms around an oil lamp to bend and focus its light into a bright ray. His magnificent apparatus could transform an oil lamp's weak light into a piercing beam visible as far as thirty miles at sea.

Fresnel built lenses in six sizes, called orders A large first-order lens served a seacoast lighthouse, while a small sixth-order lens was suitable for a river beacon. Later, titanic hyper-radiant lenses were developed for important landfall lights such as the one at Makapu'u. Fixed lenses had a smooth barrel of magnifying glass, while flashing lenses were composed of a series of magnifying bulls-eyes that broke the light into individual beams. These appeared to flash as the lens revolved, and, if timed properly, gave the lighthouse a unique signal.

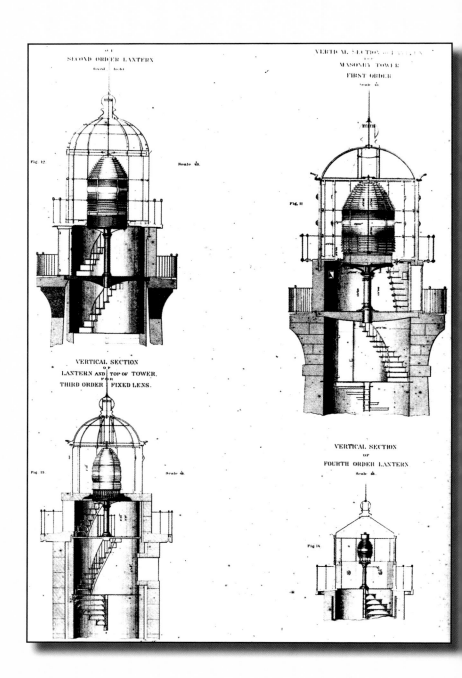

SECOND ORDER LANTERN
Fixed light

Fig. 12   Scale

VERTICAL SECTION OF LANTERN
MASONRY TOWER
FIRST ORDER
Scale

Fig. 11

VERTICAL SECTION
OF
LANTERN AND TOP OF TOWER.
FOR
THIRD ORDER FIXED LENS.

Fig. 13   Scale

VERTICAL SECTION
OF
FOURTH ORDER LANTERN
Scale

Fig. 14

XIV

Hyperradial Lens at Makapu'u, Hawai'i

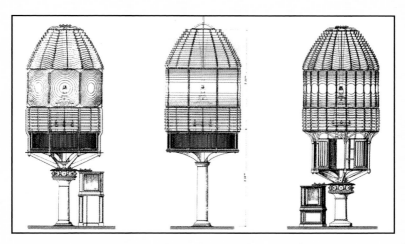

Lenses were categorized as fixed, showing a steady light (center), or flashing (left and right). Fixed lenses had a central barrel of solid magnifying glass. Lenses with bulls-eye panels produced flashes. Prisms above and below the central barrel or bulls-eyes bent light and focused it at the center of the lens. These principles of refraction and intensification of light are still used today in small plastic lenses.

Fresnel lenses were heavy and turned on bearings or chariot wheels. Larger models floated in a trough on a thin layer of mercury—a low-friction, high-density element. The mercury had to be removed and sieved regularly to keep it clean. Today, this would be considered hazardous duty because of the poisonous effects of mercury. Ironically, Lighthouse Service records do not include references to the dangers of mercury or deaths from mercury poisoning. Even children were exposed. Charles Settles of San Juan Island, Washington remembers playing with beads of escaped mercury on the lighthouse stairs of Lime Kiln Light when his father cleaned the lens trough.

A clockwork system with weights suspended in the tower, similar to a cuckoo clock mechanism, kept the lens revolving at a specified rate. The keepers wound up the weights every few hours. As the weights fell, the lens turned. During the day, keepers spent a considerable amount of time cleaning the lens and maintaining the gears of the clockworks.

Lightkeeper John Kunder of Farallon Light Station was photographed in the 1920s winding up the weights for the clockwork that turned the lens. This usually had to be done every two to four hours when the light was operating.

Oil lamps as light sources were replaced by incandescent oil vapor lamps in the 1880s, and by acetylene gas lamps in the 1890s. When electricity came to lighthouses about the turn of the twentieth century, the old Fresnel lenses were upgraded to operate with electric light bulbs. In the 1960s, automation ushered in smaller, more durable plastic lenses that worked on the same principle as the classic Fresnel lenses.

Plastic lens housings required little care and could be exposed to the weather.

Myriad sensors and timers were devised to turn the lights on and off and to rotate replacement light bulbs into position when old ones burned out. Solar panels replaced external power sources at many remote lighthouses. This progress has rendered all active lighthouses self-sufficient and made the job of the live-in lighthouse keeper obsolete. Coast Guard Aids to Navigation Teams (ANTs) still visit lighthouses periodically to check the automatic equipment. In a sense, they are lightkeepers, though their services are minimal and they need not live on-site.

The era of the lighthouse keeper, in the traditional sense, has ended. Lighthouses have become robots, able to run themselves. While such progress saves money and allows manpower to be diverted to other, more critical aspects of the Coast Guard's mission, it does render the lighthouses less romantic and charming.

A Coast Guardsman stands next to the opulent fourth-order lens of Cape Disappointment Lighthouse at the entrance to the Columbia River. The lens, which is no longer in service, used six bulls-eye panels, three of them covered in ruby glass, to create its red and white flash characteristic.

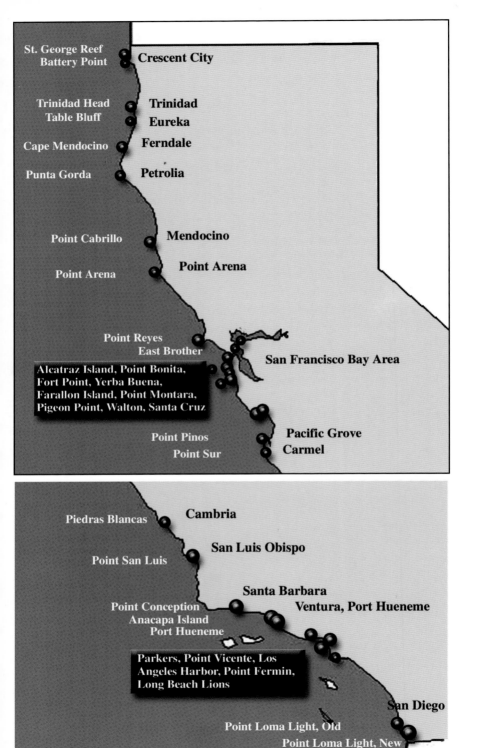

St. George Reef
Battery Point — **Crescent City**

Trinidad Head — **Trinidad**
Table Bluff — **Eureka**

Cape Mendocino — **Ferndale**

Punta Gorda — **Petrolia**

Point Cabrillo — **Mendocino**

Point Arena — **Point Arena**

Point Reyes — **Point Reyes**
East Brother

Alcatraz Island, Point Bonita,
Fort Point, Yerba Buena,
Farallon Island, Point Montara,
Pigeon Point, Walton, Santa Cruz

San Francisco Bay Area

Point Pinos — **Pacific Grove**
Point Sur — **Carmel**

Piedras Blancas — **Cambria**

Point San Luis — **San Luis Obispo**

Point Conception — **Santa Barbara**
Anacapa Island — **Ventura, Port Hueneme**
Port Hueneme

Parkers, Point Vicente, Los
Angeles Harbor, Point Fermin,
Long Beach Lions

San Diego

Point Loma Light, Old
Point Loma Light, New

XVIII

Lighthouses of California

In 1542, when Portuguese explorer Juan Rodriguez Cabrillo sailed along the coast of present-day California, he probably had no idea a lighthouse would someday bear his name. Point Cabrillo Light near Mendocino is one of more than thirty sentinels that today keep watch over the Golden State's 1,200 miles of coastline.

Other explorers, traders, whalers, and even pirates followed in Cabrillo's wake, but not until gold was discovered in California in 1848 did anyone think to build a lighthouse. As hundreds of vessels crowded into San Francisco's crude wharf area—the staging point for the overland journey into the gold fields—Congress cautiously allotted money to build lighthouses on the West Coast.

A Congressional investigation of the U.S. Lighthouse Establishment was ongoing at this time. The 60-year-old agency had come under criticism, accused of being poorly managed and inferior by worldwide standards. The lack of navigational aids on the West Coast was a major downfall of the administration.

By 1852 Congress had addressed these problems with the formation of the U.S. Lighthouse Board, a nine-member committee of military and scientific experts who met to overhaul the service and light the West Coast. They set to work immediately, and by June 1, 1854 the first California lighthouse went into operation on Alcatraz Island in San Francisco Bay. It was a Cape Cod-style structure consisting of a simple keeper's dwelling with a tower rising from the roof.

Five more California lighthouses, similar to the first, were completed in 1855, and another four were added the following year. All of the lighthouses exhibited Fresnel lenses. These French-made optics were magnificent aggregates of refracting prisms and magnifying glass held in beehive-shaped brass frames. Oil lamps placed inside the lenses served as the light source. Fresnel lenses were manufactured in various orders, or powers, with first-order lenses being the largest and sixth-order lenses being the smallest. They were state-of-the-art in the nineteenth century and considerably more expensive than other systems

1

of illumination, but their amazing ability to focus and intensify light made them worth the price.

Fog signals also were installed at many light stations to augment warnings to mariners when visibility was reduced. Early on, most fog signals were bells, but by 1880 many steam whistles, sirens, and horns were in use. They were labor-intensive devices that required much of the lightkeeper's time when the air became murky.

California's lightkeepers were hearty stock—men and women who had emigrated from the East Coast and Midwest by wagon or had made the long journey by sea, sailing around notorious Cape Horn, famed for its foul weather and rough seas. Since most light stations were situated in remote places where no roads existed, they were operated as small farms accessible primarily by boat. This allowed the keepers to subsist primarily on their own while serving the needs of the shipping industry. To entice them away from the "get rich quick" promise of the California Gold Rush, keepers on the Pacific Coast were paid more than their East Coast counterparts.

By the twentieth century the state's chain of navigational aids had grown to more than forty lighthouses. It included the nation's most expensive lighthouse at St. George Reef and two important lightships anchored off the coasts of San Francisco and Mendocino. California had become known as one of the best-marked coasts in the nation. Other navigational systems, such as radiobeacon and LORAN (Long Range Navigation), further improved the light stations. During World War II, light stations became centers of activity for beach patrols and sea watches.

Automation of California's lighthouses began in the 1950s and was completed by 1982. As the lights were unmanned and made self-sufficient, most were adopted by private, civic, or government groups who restored them and opened them to the public. Today California is the vanguard of lighthouse preservation, with two-thirds of its sentinels operating as museums or attractions in parks.

Establishing lighthouses on the wild and rugged coast of California in the 1850s was a challenge. The coast was deeply indented with harbors and coves enclosed by bold capes and headlands. Strong currents and powerful storms, coupled with the region's notorious fog, made lighting these shores a Herculean task. The Baltimore firm of Gibbons & Kelley was contracted to build twelve lighthouses, including one at remote Point Conception—a critical turning point for ships. The construction crew built a crude road to the site but most of the materials were landed by ship in a cove below the proposed sentinel and hauled up the cliff with a derrick. One item that was too heavy to be winched up the cliff was the massive fogbell. A team of oxen and horses carted it from Santa Barbara to the station. It served for almost twenty years before being replaced by a steam whistle.

Point Loma Light Station (New)   32.66N, 117.24W

FOR MORE INFORMATION

See Point Loma Lighthouse (Old)

~~~

DIRECTIONS

Follow directions for Point Loma Lighthouse (Old), then take Cabrillo Road down the bluff to the new Point Loma Light Station.

In March 1891 a pile-design, skeleton lighthouse replaced the defunct cottage-style lighthouse on top of the headland at Old Point Loma. The new lighthouse had been fabricated at Phoenix Iron Works in New Jersey, loaded piece-by-piece onto flatcars, and shipped by rail to San Diego. The name New Point Loma preserved the connection to the 1855 deactivated Old Point Loma Lighthouse on the headland.

The site chosen for the new lighthouse was Pelican Point, much lower in elevation than its predecessor and nearer the shipping lanes. The tower was assembled and bolted together on a concrete pad. Its opulent third-order Henry-LaPaute lens, which had been made in Paris and displayed at the Paris Exposition in 1887, was initially designated for use at Anclote Key Lighthouse in Florida. A change in plans in Florida resulted in the lens being assigned to New Point Loma. It had twelve bulls-eyes and operated with a kerosene lamp. It shone through windowpanes of ruby glass to differentiate it from other lights in the area.

799 – POINT LOMA LIGHT HOUSE, NEAR SAN DIEGO, CALIFORNIA

Two Victorian homes for the keepers were built behind the lighthouse, along with two privies and a catchment and cisterns for rainwater storage. Palm trees and wildflowers, along with San Diego's pleasant weather, made New Point Loma Lighthouse an ideal assignment.

The station was given a fog signal in 1913 to deal with persistent winter and spring fogs. A fog signal keeper was added to the crew, and a new house was built for him and his family. That same year, a new dwelling was built for the principal keeper, and the red panels in the lantern were removed so the light flashed white. By this time the light operated with an incandescent oil vapor lamp.

A radiobeacon was added to the station in the 1920s; electricity came in 1926. During World War II the light was extinguished and the tower was painted a dull gray-green to blend in with the trees and hillside. The lighthouse was automated in 1973 to run 24 hours a day and was upgraded with a modern optic in the 1980s. The Fresnel lens was moved to an exhibit at Cabrillo National Monument.

Coast Guard personnel still reside in the dwellings. The lighthouse is not open to the public but can be viewed from a nearby parking area.

Point Loma Light Station (Old)   32.67N, 117.24W

FOR MORE INFORMATION
Cabrillo National Monument
1800 Cabrillo Memorial Drive
San Diego, CA 92106
619.557.5450
www.nps.gov/cabr

HOURS OF OPERATION
The Visitor Center is open
daily, 9 A.M. to 5 P.M.

DIRECTIONS
Where I-8 and I-5 intersect
north of central San Diego,
take the Rosecrans Street
(Highway 209) exit and then
follow signs to Point Loma.

Established in 1855 on a promontory enclosing San Diego Harbor that Spanish explorers named for its "low, long elevation," the Point Loma Lighthouse was a simple cottage-style sentinel with the tower incorporated into the dwelling. It shone from 462 feet above sea and had a third-order Fresnel lens. While its lofty beacon was visible up to 35 miles in clear weather, winter fogs obscured the light. Yet, no fog signal was installed.

Complaints about the harbor's dense fog prompted the construction of two additional lighthouses— one at Ballast Point in 1890 and one on the beach on the west side of the promontory. Old Point Loma Light's duties were upstaged by the new sentries. It was abandoned in 1892 and stood derelict until the 1930s, when it was adopted by the National Park Service and restored as the centerpiece of Cabrillo National Monument. The site honored the Spanish explorer Juan Rodriguez Cabrillo, who sailed into San Diego in 1542.

The lighthouse is open for tours and has period furnishings that evoke the tenure of lightkeeper Robert Israel, his wife Maria, who was his official assistant, and their two sons. More recent restoration of Old Point Loma Lighthouse included installation of a third-order lens in the lantern with a low-intensity light, and exhibits inside the lighthouse and visitor center. Of special interest is the reconstructed cement catchment once used to capture rainwater.

California has several new privately built and maintained lighthouses that are included as official navigational aids on the Coast Guard's annual publication, *Light List*. The "Lions Lighthouse for Sight" was built in 2000 and is the centerpiece of an aquatic park in Long Beach. Funds to build the lighthouse were provided in part by the Long Beach Downtown Lions Club.

> **DIRECTIONS**
> From I-710 in Long Beach (I-710 becomes West Shoreline Drive), take Aquarium Way and Golden Shore Street to a parking area at Shoreline Aquatic Park, then walk to the lighthouse.

The 105-foot-tall conical steel lighthouse is a private aid to navigation and a symbol of the Lions Club's benevolent effort to aid the visually impaired. The tower is painted white, while the cage-style lantern is red. The lighthouse presides over Rainbow Harbor, is fully automatic, and serves as office space for the harbormaster of Long Beach. Windows in the base of the lighthouse allow a broad view of harbor traffic. At night the tower is floodlighted with colored lights.

The lighthouse is located just east of the Aquarium of the Pacific on the north side of the entrance to Long Beach harbor and the west side of the small boat basin. It is not open to the public.

Point Fermin Lighthouse   33.705N, 118.2936W

FOR MORE INFORMATION
Point Fermin Lighthouse
   Historic Site & Museum
807 W. Paseo Del Mar
San Pedro, CA 90731
www.pointferminlighthouse.org
310.241.0684

HOURS OF OPERATION
Tuesday through Sunday,
1 P.M. to 4 P.M.

DIRECTIONS
From I-110 South, take the
Gaffey Street exit and pro-
ceed to Point Fermin Park.

A beacon for San Pedro Bay, the Carpenter Gothic sentinel at Point Fermin operated from 1874 until 1941. Now inactive and a museum, it sits on a point named for Father Fermin Francisco de Lasuen, the head priest and overseer of several eighteenth century Franciscan missions in California.

The lighthouse was built in response to the completion of a railroad to San Pedro Bay where ships could load cargoes of redwood and fir. After Los Angeles became a major port, the importance of San Pedro Bay waned and the lighthouse was no longer needed. It was extinguished at the start of World War II and then the top portion of its lantern was rebuilt to accommodate a box-shaped lookout tower used during the war to watch for enemy activity offshore. Later it became a residence for Los Angeles City Park personnel.

Long before this time, women tended the lighthouse. Sisters Mary and Ella Smith transferred to Point Fermin Light from Ediz Hook Light in Washington. Their brother, a customs collector in Washington, was able to arrange the job for them. Ella Smith left after a few years, but Mary stayed on. Unfortunately, she was removed from the job after an assistant keeper complained about her and sought to take over her position. Later, the lighthouse was tended by sisters Thelma and Juanita Austin.

After World War II, the lighthouse deteriorated. A light on a pole close to the water had taken over its duties. Though the box-shaped tower remained on top of the roof, the structure received little care. The Coast Guard decided to tear it down, but protests from local resident forestalled the plan.

Restoration efforts began in 1974 with removal of the lookout tower and construction of a new lantern. The lighthouse's exterior and grounds were restored and the interior now serves as a museum. The historic fourth-order lens was located and returned to the lighthouse for display in one of the downstairs rooms. The Point Fermin Chapter of the U.S. Lighthouse Society manages the site and offers tours.

The clement weather of San Pedro and its nourishing ocean air made it an ideal place for gardens. Many of its keepers were women, the last being a young woman named Thelma Austin. She never married and claimed the duties she carried out were "sacred." Her feminine hands tilled the ground, planted seeds, watered, pulled weeds, and made the place a botanical paradise. When the station closed right before World War II, the gardens faded away. But in the 1980s local volunteers, including a niece of Thelma Austin, again took up trowels, hoes, and shovels and transformed Point Fermin Lighthouse into a pageant of fragrant color.

Los Angeles Harbor Lighthouse   33.708N, 118.25W

Rising from a concrete platform at the end of the 2-mile-long San Pedro Breakwater, Los Angeles Harbor Lighthouse leads the way to the West Coast's largest port. Built in 1913 at a cost of $36,000, it is sometimes called "Angel's Gate Lighthouse" for the port of "the angels."

The cylindrical tower is a one-of-a-kind design. It is constructed of twelve steel columns and plates covered in cement and painted in contrasting panels of black and white. It sits on an octagonal concrete base. A fourth-order Fresnel lens illuminated by an incandescent oil vapor lamp served as the first beacon. It revolved in a trough of low-friction mercury. Compressed-air sirens were used as the fog signal. A two-tone foghorn later replaced the sirens and

was nicknamed "Moaning Maggie" by the surrounding community.

Several traumatic incidents are recorded in the station logbook. A severe earthquake that struck Los Angeles in 1933 gave the lighthouse a jolt, but it was undamaged. The keeper reported that the tower shook and swayed, and mercury splashed out of the Fresnel lens rotation mechanism. Within months the tower shook again, this time when a Navy ship crashed into the breakwater. Storms also regularly assailed the tower. These events have caused it to lean slightly out of plumb.

The lighthouse was automated in 1973 and eventually upgraded with a modern solarized beacon, the first lighthouse on the West Coast to be powered by the sun. Its Fresnel lens was given to the Los Angeles Maritime Museum in 1990.

Parker's Lighthouse

Parker's Lighthouse is both an official lighthouse and a restaurant. Built in 1982, this privately owned and maintained sentinel is 71 feet tall and flashes white every 10 seconds. The lantern is centered at the peak of the roof on a round

DIRECTIONS
From I-170 (becomes West Shoreline Drive) look for signs for Shoreline Village. The lighthouse is on the southwestern tip of the village shops.

2½-story restaurant, known for its seafood menu. Downstairs is a lavish dining room. The small half-story area under the cupola includes a bar and lounge with dramatic views of the harbor. The architects for the lighthouse were Edmund Stevens Associates, Inc.

The lighthouse is located in Shoreline Village opposite the Long Beach Convention Center and Long Beach Lions Light. The lantern is off-limits to the public, but the restaurant area is open daily.

FOR MORE INFORMATION
www.vicentelight.org
auxstes@gmail.com
310.541.0334

HOURS OF OPERATION
Grounds are open daily dawn to dusk. The museum tours are open the second Saturday of every month 10 a.m. to 3 p.m., except March when they open the first Saturday to coincide with a local whale festival.

DIRECTIONS
From I-110 take Gaffey Street south for 2 miles to 25th Street. Turn right on 25th and drive 2.7 miles until it becomes Palos Verdes Drive. The lighthouse is another 4.5 miles.

Point Vicente Lighthouse, eight miles north of Los Angeles Harbor, marks the prominent Palos Verdes Peninsula, a turning point for ships heading for San Pedro Channel and Long Beach. Merchants and sailors began lobbying for a lighthouse here in the late nineteenth century. Plans for the lighthouse finally were approved in 1916, but a war-stressed economy put off the work for almost a decade.

The fog signal—a ten-inch chime whistle that gave two blasts a minute—went into operation first in June 1925. The Mission Revival-style, 67-foot, cylindrical concrete lighthouse first flashed its warnings seaward on April 14, 1926. At this time, the U.S. Lighthouse Board noted that 27 million tons of cargo annually passed the point, underscoring the lighthouse's importance for navigation and justifying its $100,000 price tag.

The third-order, revolving clamshell lens had been purchased from France in 1886 and used in an Alaskan lighthouse prior to its installation at Point Vicente. The focal plane of the beacon was 185 feet above the sea. By now, electricity powered many lighthouses, and Point Vicente was equipped with an electric plant to run the beacon and fog signal. A 100-watt light bulb was intensified by the lens to produce a flashing light visible some 20 miles at sea. Electricity was not wired into the dwellings, however, so keepers still cooked on coal stoves and used kerosene lamps for light.

The entire station was electrified by World War II, but blackout curtains were hung in the lantern to prevent the light from aiding enemy ships. After the war the landward panes of lantern glass were painted white to prevent the light from disturbing the many homes that had

been built on the peninsula. An after-effect of the change was an odd, hourglass-shaped reflection seen on the painted windows. The shadowy, winsome figure was nicknamed the "Lady in the Light." When the panes were repainted in 1955, the figure vanished.

The lighthouse was automated in 1971. The classical lens still flashes a warning to shipping, and the site is a popular tourist stop for whale watching. The grounds are open during daylight hours. A local Coast Guard Auxiliary offers tours of the station and has set up an exhibit in one of the buildings. Views of the lighthouse are also spectacular from the nearby Point Vicente Interpretive Center, which showcases the human and natural history of the peninsula.

Anacapa Island Lighthouse   34.015N, 119.35W

FOR MORE INFORMATION
Channel Islands National Park
1901 Spinnaker Drive
Ventura, CA 93001
805.658.5730
www.nps.gov/chis

DIRECTIONS
Boat tours to the island are offered through the park interpretive center at Channel Islands National Park in Ventura.

The volcanic remnants known as the Channel Islands include many islets and rock pinnacles, all hazardous to navigation into nearby Los Angeles Harbor. Anacapa Island, named by explorer Capt. George Vancouver for a Chumash word that roughly translates as "vanishing island," is located 14 miles off Los Angeles. It is the site of one of California's newest lighthouses.

In the 1870s an automatic acetylene gas light mounted on a skeleton tower was placed on East Island in the Anacapa chain, along with a whistling buoy anchored just offshore. The site proved too remote and expensive for a larger, staffed light station, so minor aids were built instead. The skeleton light served without censure until 1921 when a costly shipwreck occurred nearby in a dense fog. As a result, mariners demanded a better light.

In 1932 a 39-foot masonry tower replaced the gas light. The new lighthouse originally had a revolving third-order Fresnel lens made by Chance Brothers of England and visible from 25 miles. The station also had a fog signal, a dwelling, and a rainwa-

ter catchment, since there was no fresh water on the island.

In 1938 the lighthouse compound became part of Channel Islands National Monument. A year later the Coast Guard took over the site, and three families were assigned to Anacapa Lighthouse. In the early 1960s missile tests conducted at nearby Point Magu forced the automation and de-staffing of the lighthouse in 1966.

Today a modern optic does the job at Anacapa Lighthouse, and two diaphone horns mounted on a fog signal building next to the tower honk during periods of low visibility. The quarters are now occupied by Channel Islands National Park staff. The lighthouse is not open but visitors to the island can walk to it. The Fresnel lens is on display in the park visitor center.

Point Hueneme Lighthouse

The name Hueneme is from a Chumash word meaning "halfway," or "resting place." The name is apt, since the Chumash stopped at Point Hueneme in their travels up and down the Santa Barbara coast. The shore forms an elbow here and poses a danger to shipping plying the Santa Barbara Channel between the mainland and Anacapa Island.

A beautiful Victorian-style fourth-order lighthouse was established at Point Hueneme in 1874 on the south side of the port. The tower was incorporated into the dwelling. The delicate French lens was manufactured in 1897 by Barbier & Bernard. The wooden lighthouse, similar to its sister sentry at Point Fermin, served until dredging began for Port Hueneme in 1939, at which point it was sold, moved away from the point to serve as the local yacht club, and then was eventually razed.

> **FOR MORE INFORMATION**
> 310.541.0334
> www.huenemelight.org
> auxsites@gmail.com
>
> **HOURS OF OPERATION**
> Open third Saturday 10:00 A.M. to 3:00 P.M. February through October,
>
> **DIRECTIONS**
> In Port Hueneme, take Surfside Drive to the Flag Plaza (near the intersection of Surfside Drive and Ventura Road). Park in designated area follow signs for the Lighthouse Promenade, a flat, half-mile walk to the lighthouse.

The 52-foot, concrete Art Deco Moderne tower and integrated fog signal house that now stand at Point Hueneme was built in 1941, just about the time the citrus industry in California burgeoned. Quarters for the keepers were erected nearby. Dredging of the port and construction of a large wharf area meant the new lighthouse went into service on the north side of the channel at a more useful location than its predecessor. The old lens was placed in the new tower. It served until 2013 when it was replaced by a modern LED-powered optic. It will be moved downstairs in the lighthouse for display.

The lighthouse is now part of a city park. The Coast Guard opens it for tours. There are displays inside the lighthouse about its history.

Point Conception Lighthouse   34.44N, 120.46W

Known to the Spanish as the "Point of Immaculate Conception," and nicknamed the "Cape Horn of the Pacific," Point Conception is a critical turning point for ships plying the California coast. Its first lighthouse, a cottage style sentinel with keepers' quarters inside it and a first-order lens in the tower, was built in 1855 on a high bluff on the point. All materials to construct the station were brought by ship from San Francisco and then unloaded in a cove on the beach below the lighthouse. From there, they were either winched up the cliff with a derrick or taken on horseback up a serpentine trail to the lighthouse site.

The first fog signal was a huge, sonorous bell, hauled to the station in a cart pulled by two horses. It proved troublesome, because of the high elevation, and was replaced in 1872 by a steam whistle in a fog signal building about 100 feet closer to the sea.

Storms battered the lighthouse. It was also somewhat ineffective located so high above the sea. Congress allocated money in 1882 to rebuild it at a lower elevation. A granite base and brick walls strengthened the new 52-foot tower, which featured a watch room and fuel storage area. The first-order lens from the original lighthouse was

moved to the new tower.

Another dwelling was added at this time, while the remains of the old lighthouse continued to be occupied by one of the keepers for a few more years. In 1906, a spacious and comfortable new duplex was built on the hilltop behind the sentinel. Six years later another house was added and the ramshackle first dwelling was torn down.

The Coast Guard took over the station in 1939. It was automated in 1973. It continues to operate today but is not accessible to the public, because of the private ranch lands separating it from the nearest public road.

TOP: A Coast Guard Aids to Navigation crewman reprises the role of lightkeeper by cleaning lantern windows during a 2006 maintenance visit to Point Conception Lighthouse. The sentinel is in desperate need of exterior improvements, including rust removal and a new paint job.

MIDDLE: The first-order Fresnel lens at Point Conception was manufactured in Paris in 1854 at a cost of $65,000. Architects for the original lighthouse had not reckoned the optic would be so big--nearly 8 feet tall and 6 feet in diameter--and did not build the lantern large enough to accommodate it. The first keeper arrived on schedule but had no work to do while the lantern was torn down and a new, larger one was built. The magnificent lens that once produced a 1.5 million candlepower flash visible more than 20 miles was removed in 2013 and placed on display in the Santa Barbara Museum.

BOTTOM: In its heyday Point Conception Light Station was a beehive of activity. Several homes for the keepers and their large families sat on the hill above the lighthouse, connected to it by a steep wooden stairway with about 190 steps. Today little remains of the homes and the place is silent, except for the cries of seabirds and whir of wind. A dwelling built in 1912 is a shadow of its former self. A Coast Guard keeper recalled spending his honeymoon in the house in the early 1970s and waking up to a panoramic view of the Pacific out his bedroom window.

Point San Luis Light Station 35.161N, 120.75W

FOR MORE INFORMATION
San Luis Lighthouse Keepers
P.O. Box 13556
San Luis Obispo, CA 93406
805-540-5771
info@sanluislighthouse.org
www.sanluislighthouse.org

Completed in 1890 to guide shipping into the burgeoning Port of San Luis Obispo, the lighthouse was a near twin of the Victorian sentinels at Point Fermin, Ballast Point, and Point Hueneme. Today, it is one of three of these unique designs still standing in California. It takes its name from a Spanish mission established in the area in 1772 by St. Louis the Bishop, better known as Father Junipero Serra.

The wooden lighthouse had a flashing fourth-order Fresnel lens that showed a red and white signal. A steam fog signal served the needs of ships on days when the area's notorious fogbanks rolled in. It was upgraded to a compressed air horn in 1915.

Quarters for the principal keeper were in the lighthouse itself, while

two assistants lived in a duplex next door. The station was remote, dry, and windblown, with access via a rough, narrow road along the high point from the nearby settlement in San Luis Obispo Harbor. A large catchment area behind the lighthouse and a cistern caught and stored rainwater, but dry summers meant a shortage of water. Eventually, extra water was brought through a 3.5-mile pipeline from Pecho Creek.

In 1933 the station was electrified. A decade later extra personnel were assigned to the site to operate a radio station during the war, and quarters were added for them. The Coast Guard tore down the original duplex in 1961, pushed it into the ocean with a bulldozer, and replaced it with a simpler duplex for the keepers. The Fresnel lens also was upstaged that year by a modern beacon. When the station was automated with a modern optic in 1974 and the keepers were removed, the classical lens was given to the San Luis Obispo Historical Museum.

By this time the Pacific Gas & Electric Company's Diablo Canyon facility surrounded the lighthouse, preventing visitor access. The station began to deteriorate. In 1992 the Port San Luis Harbor District obtained the lighthouse from the federal government, with the stipulation that it be restored. The effort is under way, managed by the nonprofit San Luis Lighthouse Keepers.

Vehicular traffic to the site is restricted. Tours are offered by trolley and by guided hikes. Consult the website for times and fees.

The San Luis Lighthouse Keepers are slowly returning the station to its former grandeur. In 2006 (top) scaffolding enclosed the tower while restoration was done to the exterior. The quaint sentinel is one of only three Carpenter Gothic designs remaining in California.

FOR MORE INFORMATION
805-927-7361
piedrasblancastours@gmail.com
www.piedrasblancas.org

HOURS OF OPERATION
Tours are offered Tuesday, Thursday, and Saturday mornings at 10:00 A.M. Guides meet visitors at the former Piedras Blancas Motel 1.5 miles north of the station at 9:45 A.M. and run a shuttle to the site.

DIRECTIONS
At present the lighthouse is inaccessible because private lands separate it from the Coastal Highway 1. It can be viewed from the highway, one mile north of the entrance to San Simeon State Park.

Piedras Blancas Lighthouse went into service in 1875 to light a long dark space between Point Pinos and Point Conception and serve the needs of the growing lumber and whaling port at San Simeon. Piedras Blancas, meaning "white rocks" in Spanish, refers to a smattering of boulders that rise above the water just offshore of the 115-foot tower. Their white color is due to the large numbers of seabirds that inhabit the area and deposit thick layers of guano on the rocks.

The tower once exhibited a first-order Fresnel lens. A handsome duplex for the keepers and several outbuildings completed the station. In 1906 a fog signal was added. A decade after the Coast Guard took control of the lighthouse in 1939, a storm damaged the lantern, and it had to be removed. An exposed aerobeacon was installed on top of the decapitated tower. The first-order lens was given to the Cambria County Lions Club and was put on display in a faux lantern on the Pinedorado grounds in Cambria.

The light station was automated in 1975. Currently, the Bureau of Land Management, in partnership with the nonprofit Piedras Blancas Light Station Association, is restoring the station and plans to eventually fabricate a new lantern for the tower and renovate most of the buildings.

Restoration of Piedras Blancas Light Station has involved not only work on the tower and buildings, but removal of invasive plants too. A narrow path through a field of ice plant in 2005 (top) gave a hint of the work ahead for the station's many gardening volunteers. The tower's interior has been restored, as this view upward through the spiral staircase shows (bottom). The Bureau of Land Management may someday fabricate a new lantern for the topless lighthouse.

Point Sur Light Station   36.30N, 121.90W

FOR MORE INFORMATION
Central Coast Lighthouse Keepers
P. O. Box 223014
Carmel, CA 93922
831.649.7139
www.pointsur.org

HOURS OF OPERATION
Call 831.649.7139 for the current
tour times and fees.

DIRECTIONS
Point Sur is visible from Highway
1 about 19-miles south of Carmel.
Watch for signs for the turnoff to
the lighthouse parking area. Visitors must hike a steep half-mile
hill to reach the light station.

The 369-foot humpback of rock that forms Point Sur was a well-known landmark for Spanish explorers, who named it "south point." As early as 1874 the Lighthouse Board suggested a lighthouse be built at Point Sur, since it was a major landmark for mariners traveling to and from San Francisco from the south.

In 1889 it became the site of a rugged sandstone lighthouse with a flashing first-order Fresnel lens and steam whistle fog signal. A small-gauge railway brought supplies to the lighthouse and its triplex keepers' dwelling. A cistern was built to hold water for the fog signal and the dwelling. Because of the precipitous bluffs around the light station, a fence enclosed the complex, while a wooden platform served as a makeshift pasture for the lightkeepers' cow.

Powerful storms assailed the point with storm surges that sometimes washed over the low flats connecting the point to the mainland. Fogs were a problem too. For this reason, the lighthouse was built at a lower elevation than the rest of the station to shine its light below the fog line.

When the station was automated in 1972 the lens was removed and given to the Maritime Museum of Monterey. It was replaced by an aero-marine beacon. The foghorn at this time was a diaphone horn. It was later discontinued.

When Point Sur State Park was established, the lighthouse reservation was included in the park. The sentinel and its remaining buildings were slowly refurbished and opened for tours courtesy of the Central Coast Lighthouse Keepers. In 2004 the light station was officially transferred to California State Parks under the National Historic Lighthouse Preservation Act.

The hulking rock known as Point Sur, having caused numerous calamities at sea, was considered a critical location for a lighthouse when settlement began in California in the 1850s. Lack of funding and difficulties accessing the site stalled construction of a lighthouse until 1889. The rugged sandstone tower originally operated with a first-order Fresnel lens fueled by whale oil. Today a modern, double, rotating, aero-marine beacon does the job. The rock has a tenuous connection to the mainland in the form of a flat, sandy spit called a tombolo (Italian for mound). It formed as the shallows around the rock slowed and refracted incoming waves, forcing them to wrap around it and converge on the opposite side, depositing sediment.

Point Pinos Lighthouse   36.63N, 121.93W

FOR MORE INFORMATION
Point Pinos Lighthouse
Asiloman Blvd. & Lighthouse Ave.
Pacific Grove, CA 93950
831.648.3179

HOURS OF OPERATION
The museum is open in winter Thursday through Monday, 1 P.M. to 4 P.M. Extended hours are offered in summer.

DIRECTIONS
From Highway 1 in Monterey, turn west on SR 68. Take Sunset Drive, then turn right on Asilomar Avenue. Follow signs to the lighthouse.

Established in 1855 to mark the entrance to Monterey Bay, little Point Pinos Light is the oldest continuously operating lighthouse on the West Coast. The name Punta de los Pinos, bestowed in 1602 by Spanish explorer Sebastian Vizcaino, means "Point of Pines."

The lighthouse went into service with a third-order lens fueled by whale oil lamps. An unusual eclipser in the form of a hammered copper panel revolved around the light source, causing the light to be obscured for 10 seconds and then visible for 20 seconds. Fuel sources changed, first to lard oil, then kerosene by 1880, then incandescent oil vapor about 1900, and finally electricity in 1915.

Writer and poet Robert Louis Stevenson, who was trained in marine engineering and was the grandson of a famous Scottish lighthouse builder, visited Point Pinos Lighthouse in 1879. He played the lighthouse piano, admired the keeper's artwork and fastidiousness, and dined with him.

For many years the station was tended by women. First, Charlotte Layton took over in 1860 upon her husband's death. Then Emily Fish, the mother-in-law of a Lighthouse Service inspector, served for many years, beginning in 1893 (see following pages). She was on duty when the lighthouse was jolted by the 1906 San Francisco earthquake, which rocked the lens and sent a large crack up the tower wall. Afterward, the structure underwent extensive repairs.

When the lighthouse was automated in 1975, the Pacific Grove Historical Society began operating it as a museum. In 2006 the Coast Guard transferred the property to the city of Pacific Grove. The tower's third order lens still shines over the bay but also over a modern golf course.

The Socialite Lightkeeper

Lighthouse keeping was, by and large, an arduous occupation held by men. Men designed the lighthouses and built, repaired, and tended them. When lightkeepers died, sometimes their wives or daughters were given the job. It was easier to appoint a widow or other female relative than to train a new man, and cheaper because women seldom earned equal pay. Yet in this male-dominated world, a few unusual ladies rose to prominence. Emily Fish was one of them.

Mrs. Fish learned social graces as a young girl in Michigan, and she married well. Her physician husband practiced medicine in China for many years and returned to the United States in 1862 with Emily and their daughter, Julia. The girl, actually Emily's niece, had been adopted when her mother died. Dr. Fish attended the sick and injured during the Civil War as a Union officer, then was transferred to the Army Installation at Benecia in San Francisco.

When he died in 1893, fifty-year-old Emily began to look for activities to fill her time. There were charities in need of help—a wealthy widow would have been expected to do volunteer work—or she could open a millinery or dress shop. But Mrs. Fish set her sights on something more engaging. Her son-in-law, Henry Nichols, was the lighthouse district inspector in California. He soon made arrangements for her to have the lightkeeping job at Point Pinos Lighthouse in Pacific Grove. She took charge of the station on June 29, 1893 and remained on duty for twenty-one years.

During those years she gained a reputation not only as an excellent lighthouse keeper but also a Monterey socialite. Mrs. Fish planted beautiful gardens at the lighthouse and kept champion livestock, which her Chinese servant, Que, helped her tend. She held teas and dinners in her home, and when she drove her carriage into town to attend a high-society event, a French poodle sat on a velvet cushion at her side.

Emily was always fashionably dressed, even as she went about her lighthouse duties. She wrote verbose entries in her logbook describing the lighthouse work, but she also wrote about such things as rainbows, meteor showers, and the appearance of Halley's Comet in 1910. On May 8, 1906, she wrote a terse but clear entry about the earthquake that had rocked the station: "Earthquake at 11:40 p.m., quite severe. Lens, etc. jostled, rattled, jingled."

Lightkeeping must have been in the family genes, for after Mrs. Fish's daughter was widowed, she also became a lighthouse keeper and served many years at San Francisco Bay's Angel Island Light. Like her mother, she was dedicated to her work. On one occasion when the fogbell striker broke down, Julia rang the bell by hand for several days until a repairman arrived to fix the striker.

Mrs. Fish retired in 1914 with a Letter of Commendation from the Department of Commerce. She and Que moved to a quiet home in Pacific Grove. She died at the age of 88 and is buried in Oakland with her daughter and son-in-law.

Santa Cruz Lighthouse   36.95N, 122.026W

FOR MORE INFORMATION
Santa Cruz Surfing Museum
1305 East Cliff Drive
Santa Cruz, CA 95062
santacruzsurfingmuseum.org
831.420.6289

HOURS OF OPERATION
Open Wednesday through Monday, July 4 through Labor Day, from 10 A.M. to 5 P.M. In winter, hours are Thursday through Monday 12 P.M to 4 P.M

DIRECTIONS
From Santa Cruz Beach Boardwalk take West Cliff Drive. The lighthouse is easy to spot and there is ample parking.

The first lighthouse at Santa Cruz was a wooden cottage-style sentinel built in 1869 on the west side of the harbor. It was a twin to the Ediz Hook Lighthouse in Washington. The pastoral, 10-acre station had vegetable and flower gardens, orchards, and livestock in surrounding fields. A quaint fifth-order Fresnel lens illuminated by lard oil lamps provided the beacon. The name Santa Cruz honored the nearby settlement known in Spanish as "Holy Cross."

The first keeper, a preacher named Adna Hecox, had brought his family west on a wagon train in 1846 and settled in Santa Cruz, where he became a respected citizen in the community and the natural choice for the lighthouse job. Only a decade into his tenure, erosion threatened the lighthouse when sea caves were discovered underneath it. The comely structure was removed from its foundation and placed on rollers. Teams of horses pulled it to a new location about 300 feet north of its original position.

Hecox's daughter, Laura, took over as keeper upon his death in 1883. In 1913 she hosted

Old Santa Cruz Lighthouse

Laura Hecox

workmen who came to the station to replace the fifth-order lens with a more powerful fourth-order optic that would not be outshone by the lights of the growing city behind it. The new lens had an occulting signal.

Erosion continued to plague the point and again threatened the lighthouse. In 1941 the Coast Guard abandoned the old sentinel and moved the light to a 26-foot wooden framework tower with a simple lens-lantern. The old lighthouse was used as a residence during World War II. In 1948 it was torn down.

The current brick lighthouse at Santa Cruz was built in 1967 as a family memorial honoring eighteen-year-old Mark Abbott, who drowned off the point while surfing. The lantern came from the defunct Oakland Harbor Lighthouse. The lighthouse is home to the Santa Cruz Surfing Museum.

Walton Lighthouse

36.96N, 122.002W

The lighthouse is not open for tours but can be viewed from the Santa Cruz Marina or from the adjacent beach. It can be reached on foot via a breakwater.

California's newest lighthouse was built in 2001 on the West Jetty of Santa Cruz and dedicated on June 9, 2002. The Walton Lighthouse replaced a characterless, cylindrical, fiberglass beacon that local residents had dubbed "The Water Heater." The new lighthouse, also called the Santa Cruz Harbor Light, is much comelier than its predecessor and much taller too. The 45-foot tapering tower was named for one of its patrons, Charles Walton, who donated $60,000 for the project in memory of his brother, who served in the Merchant Marines. It is a steel plate tower that exhibits a modern green optic 54 feet above the sea. It has never had a keeper but operates automatically.

Spend the Night at a Light

As lighthouses were automated and de-staffed by the Coast Guard in the 1980s, new uses were found for them. One popular transformation made lighthouses into overnight lodging. The lure of spending a night under the light and walking in the footsteps of yesterday's lightkeepers proved a profitable attraction that maintained a human presence at lighthouses and also provided a stream of income for their upkeep. After all, the word lighthouse contains the word house, suggesting someone ought to reside there, if only for a short vacation.

Elegant accommodations at
East Brother Light Station

Keepers' quarters at a number of light stations now serve as B&Bs, hostels, or vacation rentals. Accommodations range from the elegant rooms and multicourse meals at Heceta Head Lighthouse and East Brother Light Station to the basic and comfortable furnishings in the Point Arena Lighthouse dwellings and Browns Point Light's little cottage. Point Cabrillo Light and Point Robinson Light have period furnishings. North Head Light's dwellings

31

overlook the stormy Pacific from a high cliff. Those looking for cheaper and simpler accommodations can use the switch-dorm style hostels at Pigeon Point Lighthouse and Point Montara Lighthouse.

One of the more unique experiences in lighthouse lodging is offered at New Dungeness Light Station on the Strait of Juan de Fuca, Washington. The 1857 lighthouse sits in a wildlife refuge at the end of a long sand spit facing British Columbia. It is accessed only by foot, or at low tide in the station's special four-wheel vehicles (above). No other vehicular traffic is permitted.

"Keepers," as the volunteer staff call themselves, have one-week assignments at the site. They live in the modernized 1904 dwelling and do regular maintenance, upkeep, and public tours. Visitors arrive on foot, trekking eleven miles roundtrip to see the historic lighthouse, or by kayak or canoe across Dungeness Bay. Thanks to the resident staff, they can climb the tower, tour the small interpretive center, and have a picnic on the lawn. There is a restroom and fresh water on the grounds. Volunteer keepers are on duty 365 days a year.

Though the beacon at New Dungeness Light Station operates automatically, volunteer crews have plenty of work to do to keep the station shipshape. At the same time, they can relax in the comfortable dwelling, which sleeps ten, with books, puzzles, and other restful activities (opposite page). There's even satellite TV for those who want to keep in touch with the mainstream world. The kitchen is well equipped. The views over the strait and toward the Olympic Mountains are spectacular.

New Dungeness Light Station was one of the first in the nation to transfer its daily duties from U.S. Coast Guard keepers to volunteer civilian keepers. It began this tradition in 1994 and considers the effort a special form of "living history." The Coast Guard maintains the beacon; volunteers take care of everything else. Perhaps the best part of the endeavor is the camaraderie and shared commitment of saving an important piece of history.

Volunteer keepers at New Dungeness 365 days a year.

For more information on becoming a volunteer lightkeeper at New Dungeness Light Station visit www.newdungenesslighthouse.com.

Pigeon Point Light Station   37.18N, 122.39W

FOR MORE INFORMATION
Pigeon Point Light Station
  State Historic Park
www.parks.ca.gov/?page_id=533
Park Office: 650.879.2120
Hostel Info: 650.879.0633

HOURS OF OPERATION
Daytime visitors welcome 8
A.M. until sunset.

DIRECTIONS
The station can be spotted
easily 5 miles south of the
Pescadero turnoff from Coastal
Highway 1.

Named for the clipper ship *Carrier Pigeon*, which wrecked off the point in 1853, stately Pigeon Point Lighthouse went into service in 1873 to provide a first-order seacoast light for vessels headed north to San Francisco. The 115-foot tower shares the distinction of being the tallest tower on the West Coast with Point Arena Lighthouse.

The original layout of the station included a quadraplex Victorian house for the keepers and a whistle house for the fog signal, which had a complex signature consisting of a four-second blast, seven seconds of silence, another four second blast, and then 45-seconds of silence. The opulent first-order lens was manufactured in Paris by the lens company Henry-LaPaute and contained 1,008 prisms. It served first at Cape Hatteras Lighthouse in North Carolina but was removed during the Civil War and placed in storage. After the war it was shipped to California for use at Pigeon Point.

Lightkeepers at Pigeon Point often gave tours of the station, impeccably dressed in full dress uniform. At least one keeper indulged in a bit of hyperbole to impress his guests. A local newspaper reported in

1883: "Our escort was of a very talkative disposition and took great pride in dilating upon the wonders of the establishment. As we stood inside the immense lens which surrounds the lamp, he startled us by stating in impressive tones that, were he to draw the curtains from the glass, the heat would be so great that the glass would melt instantly, and that human flesh would follow suit; we begged him not to experiment just then, and he kindly refrained."

The Coast Guard razed the dwelling and replaced it with bungalows in 1960s. The lighthouse was automated in 1979 and shortly after that it was licensed to the California Department of Parks and Recreation. Hostelling International/American Youth Hostels operates the station as a hostel for travelers.

Montara is the surname of a family that settled in Central California during the mission era. The Montara family lent their name to several landmarks, including a point on the seacoast in western San Mateo County and its lighthouse.

Heavy fogs that caused trouble for San Francisco-bound shipping spurred construction of a steam fog whistle in 1875 at Point Montara, about 25 miles south of the Golden Gate. The signal was a 12-inch steam whistle that gave a 5-second blast every 30 seconds. The boiler that provided the steam for the fog signal gobbled up between 75 and 100 tons of coal a year.

In 1900 a small kerosene post light was added to the site. Its red beacon was visible for 12 miles. This was upgraded in 1912 to a fourth-order Fresnel lens mounted in a wooden framework tower. By this time a newer, more powerful fog signal had been installed and two keepers resided on the station in a Victorian-style dwelling.

Finally, in 1928 the present 30-foot cast-iron lighthouse was

built. The conical iron tower had formerly served at Mayo's Beach, Cape Cod beginning in 1881. When it was discontinued there, it was dismantled and shipped to the Lighthouse Depot at Yerba Buena, California. From there it was sent south to Point Montara.

In the 1950s Coast Guard bungalows were added to the station. The lighthouse was automated in 1970 with a modern optic, and its classical lens was removed and put on display at San Mateo County Historical Museum. The fog signal machinery was shut down when an offshore buoy took over its duties.

In the 1980s a hostel opened, with the staff housed in the old Victorian keepers' quarters. Dorms for overnight guests were opened in the bungalows and the fog signal building. A display of the station's history and local lore also is housed in the fog signal building. The grounds are open to visitors a few hours each day, depending on the season and weather. Hours are posted on a sign at the entrance.

Though lighthouses and their ancillary structures were built on a strict budget and were meant to be entirely functional, hints of architectural beauty are present. The Victorian-style dwelling at Point Montara Light Station is a good example. Steep dormers, ornate windows, and gingerbread trim combine in this practical but handsome building. Today it serves as quarters for the staff of the station's youth hostel.

Farallon Island Lighthouse

FOR MORE INFORMATION
Farallon National Wildlife Refuge
1 Marshlands Road
Fremont, CA 94555
510.792.0222
sfbaynwrc@fws.gov

The Farallon Islands are about 23 miles off the coast of San Francisco. The name means "brothers" in Spanish. A squat brick lighthouse went into operation on the summit of Southeast Farallon Island in 1855, more than 2,000 feet above sea level. A switchback trail, plied by the lightkeepers and their donkeys, led from the lighthouse down to the quarters and work buildings. Another, less steep trail led to the two boat landings.

The light's purpose was to guide shipping into San Francisco and help coastal vessels avoid the dreaded rocks off the Farallon Islands. The station's original optic was a first-order Fresnel lens that cast a beam about 20 miles seaward. The first fog signal was an experimental train whistle mounted over a natural blowhole and actuated by the concussion of air. It proved unreliable and was replaced by a steam siren in 1882.

During its early days, the station was plagued by egg hunters from San Francisco who gathered the island's many seabird eggs from the rookeries on its steep slopes. These were sold to bakeries in the city. At least one light-keeper also operated a profitable side business gathering and selling eggs, until the Lighthouse Service banned the work.

A weather station was established on Farallon Island in the early 1900s, along with a radio compass station. During World War II the island was critical to military operations and had a population of more than fifty people, keepers included. In the 1960s the lantern of the lighthouse was removed and an aero-marine beacon was installed. The station was automated in 1972 with a modern optic.

Today Farallon Island Light is part of the Point Reyes Farallon Island National Marine Sanctuary. Though the island is off limits to visitors, special tour boats visit the waters around the island on weekends from June through November. During marine mammal and bird migrations, researchers reside in the old quarters and conduct studies.

Yerba Buena Lighthouse

Yerba Buena Island, named "good herb" by the Spanish for a healthful plant that grew on its slopes, was home to the Lighthouse Service Depot that served the Thirteenth Lighthouse District. The depot had storehouses, workshops, and a wharf where lighthouse tenders tied up. It seemed only fitting that a lighthouse was built on its southeast shore in 1875. While the island was popularly called Goat Island at the time, its Spanish name was revived in the 1930s and continues today.

The small, octagonal wooden tower with quaint green trim exhibited a fixed fourth-order light. A large fog signal building below the lighthouse held two 10-inch steam whistles, while a fogbell served as a backup if the steam system failed in San Francisco's relentless murk. Above the tower near the hilltop was a beautiful gabled keepers' duplex. Proximity of the depot made life easier for the keepers, since supplies and repairmen were close at hand.

In 1936 the island was dwarfed by the Trans-Bay Bridge and its connecting tunnel that carried traffic through the island. That same year floodlights were added to the grounds to make the lighthouse more visible to ships. Automation came in 1958, though the Fresnel lens was not removed and remains in service today.

The attractive keepers' dwelling is now the home of a Coast Guard admiral. The lighthouse, on government property, is not open to the public. It can be seen from ferries running to Oakland and also from tour boats that depart from Fisherman's Wharf.

1706 – Light House, Yerba Buena Island, San Francisco Bay, California.

Four-Footed Keepers

Few lighthouse families were without pets. Animals eased the loneliness of isolated duty and provided important services.

Cats kept down the rodent population—no small service considering the many wooden buildings at light stations. Their natural agility allowed them to climb the towers without fear and dispatch bugs drawn to the light. Island felines swam to shore to visit other cats or stowed away on ships that visited the light stations. This happened to the cat belonging to the Coast Guard crew at Los Angeles Harbor Lighthouse in the 1960s. A buoy tender stopped to supply the lighthouse, which sits at the harbor entrance on the tip of a long breakwater. The tender departed, then was observed to make a wide turn and head back to the lighthouse. As it came alongside, the keepers saw their cat in the arms of one of the buoy tender's crew. She had sneaked onto the vessel, hoping to take a little vacation from lighthouse duties.

A cat named Jiggs lived at several California lighthouses. He was born under the back porch of the quarters at Pigeon Point

Lighthouse in the spring of 1927. When Keeper Tom Henderson was transferred to Point Sur Lighthouse in 1930, his family took Jiggs with them. Though cats often live well into the teen years, Jiggs died suddenly at age nine. The Hendersons buried him in a cat-sized concrete crypt on the bluff below the lighthouses and inscribed it: Jiggs Apr.22, 1927—Dec. 20, 1936. A few years later the Hendersons transferred to Point Pinos Lighthouse.

Unable to leave the deceased Jiggs behind, they dug up his crypt and carted it to their new home. He was re-interred in a quiet area of the lighthouse lawn. A cross marks the spot today.

Sometimes the receding tide influenced a lighthouse cat's urge to roam, when the isthmus separating the lighthouse from the mainland was no longer covered by water. This happened daily at Battery Point Lighthouse in Northern California. Caretakers Jerry and Nadine Tugel had several cats living with them in the 1980s and 1990s, including a pair of Turkish Vans, felines known for their love of water. The two kitties, named Samuel and Jeffrey, weren't opposed to getting their paws wet and often went ashore when the tide went out, "in search of excitement," said Nadine Tugel. Each had a marine calendar in his head though, and seemed to know when to return. Just as the tide turned and the isthmus between the lighthouse and shore began to disappear, they would quickly cross, picking their way over rocks not yet submerged.

Dogs were indispensable at lighthouses. They guarded the stations, watching for ships in distress, an intruder, a child in danger. Large breeds, such as Newfoundlands, were prized for their love of water and their rescue skills. In the 1920s a dog at Cape Flattery Lighthouse swam out to fetch the mail from the canoe-paddling carrier. The dog's courage often averted disaster for "Lighthouse Charley," the postman from the Makah Reservation at Neah Bay. Even on calm days Charley's canoe could be smashed on the rocks rimming the island.

Smaller dogs had important roles too. Most were good ratters and discouraged seabirds from landing on and fouling the buildings. Anacapa Island Lighthouse had as many as thirteen little dogs in the 1950s, mostly beagles. The hounds had a special purpose. A pair of Belgian hares that were pets of Coast Guard keepers had escaped from the house years before, multiplied, and overran the island, digging holes everywhere. The beagles must have thought they were in heaven when they arrived and were turned

loose. They eradicated the rabbits, and the keepers filled in the holes. Mission accomplished, most of the beagles were returned to shore, but several favorites were kept as pets.

Dogs sometimes served lightkeepers in even more peculiar ways. At Yaquina Head Lighthouse in the 1920s, an assistant keeper named Frank Story would only go to the tower when accompanied by his bulldog. The tower was reputedly haunted by the ghost of an earlier keeper. Story felt his dog would protect him from the wraith.

The most critical animals at lighthouses were those with hooves and feathers. Cows and goats did their share to provide the lighthouse families with milk and cheese. Chickens provided eggs and meat for the table. Goats kept the brush and grass at a manageable height. Even in modern times this is true: Point Robinson Lighthouse on Vashon-Mary Island in Puget Sound sees rent-a-goats from time to time, brought to the station to eat down the blackberry bramble.

A barn and chicken coop were integral parts of the light station architecture. The Lighthouse Service wanted lighthouse families to be as self-sufficient as possible, so many light stations doubled as small farms. Logbooks mention these structures on occasion, as when a chicken coop blew down in a strong Pacific storm and had to be rebuilt or a cow escaped from her barn and pasture and ended up in trouble. This happened at Point Cabrillo Lighthouse in the 1920s when the station cow fell down the cliff at the edge of the compound and was stranded on an outcropping. The keeper drove his car to the cliff and hooked a rope around the cow, then pulled her to safety with the car. In a similar incident, a bull at Cape Flattery Light disappeared in January 1921 and was feared lost at sea. Later he was found swimming ashore, obviously after having fallen. The keepers were so pleased to have him back they rewarded him with extra grain and hay.

Horses, mules, and oxen not only helped build the light stations but often stayed on to serve the keepers in a variety of ways. These large animals were transported to island lighthouses by the supply ships and were lifted in a sling onto the dock of their new home. Sometimes they were pushed into the sea close to the island and swam ashore. These experiences often were traumatic, leaving the beleaguered beasts seasick and bawling, but grateful to have their hooves on dry land once again.

At Farallon Island Lighthouse a steep trail led from the north and south boat landings, to the fog signal house, past the residences, and up to the light tower. A 3,559-foot narrow gauge railway with a tramcart covered part of the trail. Mules had helped in the construction of the station, including the little railway, and one was left on site to serve the keepers. The station mule was listed as a member of the crew carrying the duties of pulling provisions to the homes and coal to the fog signal house in a small rail car. Supplies for the tower, including containers of fuel, were backpacked up a long switchback trail to the island's summit.

One of the best-known Farallon mules was Jerry, a smart character who always heard the whistle of the supply ship long before the keepers did. Its distant, shrill cry usually sent Jerry hastily retreating to the far end of the island to hide, since he knew the arrival of the ship meant he'd be harnessed to the tramcart and forced to work for hours. When Jerry died on Christmas night in 1874 the keepers were inconsolable. They carved a headstone for him that simply read *Jerry*, and noted in the logbook that he held the distinction of having lived on Farallon Island longer than any other Lighthouse Service resident. He truly was Farallon Light Station's first keeper.

A docile jenny mule named Patty arrived at Farallon Island Light station in 1885 on the tender *Madrono*. Her companion was a horse named Jenny. Both were much loved by the lighthouse children of keepers William Beeman and Cyrus O'Caine. The children dressed them in funny hats and rode them about the island. The two often starred in the children's plays and reenactments of terrible storms, shipwrecks, and pirate attacks. By this time a blacksmith shop had been added to the light station, principally to provide shoes for the equines. At Christmas, when the tender arrived with a tree and gifts the keepers had ordered, there was always something for Patty and Jenny too—carrots and apples drizzled with honey or rolled in sugar. Patty was even included in a family portrait taken outside the dwelling about 1889. She died at the station and was buried there. A keeper wrote a poetic tribute to her—

Mule Patty. Always good,
Caused no trouble where she stood,
Always ready and seldom sick,
Died of age without a kick.

Mule Patty, "Always Good."

Fort Point Lighthouse   37.81N, 122.47W

FOR MORE INFORMATION
Fort Point National Historic Site
Fort Mason, Building 201
San Francisco, CA 94123
www.nps.gov/fopo
415.556.1693

HOURS OF OPERATION
Open weekends Friday through
Sunday 10 A.M. to 5 P.M.

DIRECTIONS
From Lincoln Boulevard in San
Francisco, turn north at Long
Avenue and follow signs to the
Fort Point National Historic
Site.

Beneath the south anchorage of the Golden Gate Bridge is the diminutive Fort Point Lighthouse. No longer functional as a navigation aid, it originally worked in tandem with the Lime Point Light, a minor beacon on a pole on the north shore of the Golden Gate. Together, the lights marked the bottleneck entrance to San Francisco Bay.

The first sentinel located at Fort Point was a cottage-style design with a stubby tower and lantern rising from the roof. While awaiting delivery of its lens in 1854, the Army chose the point for a fort, and construction began. Army buildings soon obscured the lighthouse, so it was torn down before ever going into operation, and a wooden light tower was erected between the fort and the bay. It became operational with a fifth-order Fresnel lens in March 1855.

After erosion destroyed the wooden tower, the third and current lighthouse was built on the fort wall in 1864. The modest 27-foot steel light tower perched on the fort's northwest wall. It served for sixty-three years before it was discontinued in 1937 when lights and foghorns on the bridge deck superseded it. Today the unused lighthouse is part of Fort Point National Historic Site.

The Golden Gate Bridge under construction in about 1935 dwarfed the little Fort Point Lighthouse, seen behind a telephone pole near the center of the photo. Lights and fog signals on the bridge deck rendered the lighthouse unnecessary.

Point Bonita Lighthouse   37.815N, 122.52W

FOR MORE INFORMATION
www.nps.gov/goga

HOURS OF OPERATION
Tours are offered Saturday through Monday, 12:30 P.M. to 3:30 P.M.. There also are occasional full-moon tours. For times call 415.331.1540.

DIRECTIONS
On the north side of the Golden Gate Bridge, take the Alexander Avenue exit to Marin Headlands, then drive through a tunnel and onto Conzelman Road, following signs to the Point Bonita parking area. Walk one mile to the lighthouse.

Perched on precipitous cliffs 306 feet above the sea on the northern entrance to San Francisco Bay, the Point Bonita Light Station began service in 1855 on a tenuous finger of land the Spanish named "beautiful point." The 56-foot conical tower stood on the highest part of the point, with a trail that led southeast to a simple 1½-story stone dwelling. Point Bonita Light exhibited a second-order Fresnel lens.

The fog signal was a cannon fired twice an hour. It was the West Coast's first fog signal, yet it was too arduous and costly to operate in San Francisco's notorious murk. In 1858 it was replaced by a 1,500-pound bell. As if to augur future problems at the site, the bell's low bong caused pieces of rock to loosen from the cliff and tumble into the sea.

Erosion and landslides constantly plagued the station and gnawed at the lighthouse foundation. The tower, which had been unknowingly built above the fog line, was in danger of collapse by 1870. It was rebuilt in 1877 at a lower elevation closer to the shipping lane. The new squat lighthouse with attached service room sat on a concrete-faced rock ledge 124 feet above the sea at the extreme southwesterly part of the point. The original second-order lens was moved to the new sentinel.

A trail and a 118-foot tunnel, hand dug by Chinese laborers, led to the somewhat cramped home on the cliff, inhabited by two keepers and their families and a bachelor keeper. A windmill for pumping water from a spring and a 12,000-gallon cistern also were built to provide steam for the new fog siren and household water. There was a coal bin for fuel storage for the fog signal. To facilitate communication between the lighthouse, fog siren building, and the dwellings, a call bell was installed.

The fog signal, which was perhaps the most critical function at the station, had been problematic for years, due to the harsh weather on the point and landslides. In 1903, a new brick fog signal building was constructed about 20 feet seaward of the lighthouse and the boilers were fitted up to use both coal and oil.

Meanwhile, the assistants and their families moved into the old fog signal building and used it as dwelling. It was crowded and damp. Finally, in 1908 and 1915, two spacious new dwellings were built for the assistants. A decade later the entire station was electrified, including the fog signal. This reduced the amount of work and the number of keepers needed.

Erosion and a powerful storm in 1940 cut a swath between the lighthouse and the shore. While a short causeway was built over the ravine, the keepers used a breeches buoy to reach the lighthouse. In 1954 the causeway was replaced by a charming little suspension bridge, painted white. Also at this time the old dwellings were burned down and the Coast Guard replaced them with bungalows.

The station was the last manned lighthouse in California when it was automated in 1981. It transferred from the Coast Guard to the Golden Gate National Recreation Area. Park rangers occupy the Coast Guard bungalows today. The beacon still signals to vessels approaching San Francisco.

Alcatraz Island Lighthouse   37.82N, 122.42W

FOR MORE INFORMATION
goga_alcatraz@nps.gov
www.nps.gov/alcatraz

DIRECTIONS
The lighthouse is accessible by boat from Pier 41 near Fisherman's Wharf. The tower is not open for climbing, but visitors touring the prison can go to the base of the lighthouse.

In 1775, Spanish explorer Manuel de Ayala sailed into San Francisco Bay and named Alcatraz Island, which translates as "Isle of the Pelicans." The lighthouse on the island, established on June 1, 1854, was the first sentinel to go into service on the West Coast. The two-story, cottage-style structure had a short lantern rising from its roof and a third-order fixed Fresnel lens with a range of 19 miles. Two years later, after other lighthouses had gone in service on the approach to San Francisco, the optic was changed to a flashing fourth-order lens.

Also at this time, a fogbell was added on the island's south shore. It was struck by hand at first—an onerous task given San Francisco's frequent and persistent fogs. Eventually, an automatic striking mechanism was installed with a clockwork system and weights to run it.

By 1856 the lighthouse shared the island with a fort and a few years later a military prison. Little by little, more buildings were constructed until by the late nineteenth century a small city existed on Alcatraz Island. Captain R. Leeds, lightkeeper in the 1880s, opened a small post office in the lighthouse basement.

In 1909 construction was begun on a maximum security prison. Its buildings would dwarf the diminutive lighthouse and so a new tower was designed. The 84-foot reinforced concrete lighthouse with an electric arc light went into operation on the island's south slope. The beacon shone from an imposing perch 214 feet above the bay. Electric fog sirens also were installed on the north and south shores of the island.

The light was automated in 1963 and quietly slipped into self-sufficient operations, but a few years later it was in the news. In 1970, during the Native American occupation of the island as a protest against loss of tribal lands, the keeper's quarters were burned. Electricity to the island was cut off in an attempt to coerce occupiers to leave. It left a dark space in San Francisco Bay and shipping interests started their own protest. The oc-

cupiers demanded they be allowed to staff and operate the lighthouse. After 19 months of occupation, the dispute ended, electricity was restored to the island, and the lighthouse returned to normal operations.

Today the lighthouse functions with a modern beacon and is run by remote control from the Coast Guard station at Fort Point. It is part of Golden Gate National Recreation Area. The keeper's quarters were never rebuilt but the walls remain.

East Brother Light Station   37.96N, 122.43W

FOR MORE INFORMATION
East Brother Light Station
117 Park Place
Point Richmond, CA 94801
510.233.2385
www.ebls.org

DIRECTIONS
For directions to the boat landing in Point Richmond visit
www.ebls.org.

The quaint Victorian light-house on East Brother Island, about a half-mile from Point Richmond, has stood watch over the entrance to San Pablo Strait since March 1874. It is situated on one of the larger rocks in a group known as The Brothers. The 48-foot wooden tower was incorporated into the keeper's house, which is of Carpenter Gothic style. A fourth-order revolving Fresnel lens still casts a beam about 10 miles over the bay.

Three months after the light went into service a steam whistle was installed to penetrate the dense fog of the area. Water for the whistle's steam boiler was brought at first by ship and pumped ashore to a tank. Later, a domed cement cistern that took up most of the island was built to collect rainwater or accept water brought out by ship.

The station logbook recorded a number of important events including the 1906 San Francisco earthquake, which damaged the station. A worse event occurred in November 1939 when a lamp was knocked over accidentally and set fire to the boathouse. The ensuing blaze destroyed part of the station.

In 1967 the station was automated with a modern, self-sufficient beacon. A few years later the Coast Guard abandoned the lighthouse and announced plans to demolish it. A local group quickly filed paperwork to have the station admitted to the National Register of Historic Places, which saved it. The East Brother Light Station Association, Inc. formed in 1979 and began work on the old sentinel. It was restored and opened as a bed and breakfast.

Today the station is accessible by boat for day trips or for overnight stays. Visitors enjoy the nostalgic firing of the old fog signal, now replaced by a modern horn. A fourth-order Fresnel lens, similar to the original, is on display in the lighthouse. There are five overnight guest rooms.

Considered one of the foggiest and windiest places on the West Coast, Point Reyes—the "point of the kings" in Spanish—was marked with a lighthouse in 1870. Construction of the station was arduous, with building materials landed by ship on Drake's Beach and then hauled up to the cliff by derrick and carted by oxen to the 120-acre light station. A niche for the light tower was dynamited into the rock face 300 feet below the top of the cliff. The squat, 35-foot tall, 16-sided cast-iron tower— a sister sentry in design to the lighthouse at Cape Mendocino—showed a first-order, three-ton, French-made lens from a ledge 294 feet above sea level. The beacon flashed once every 5 seconds.

A comfortable duplex for the keepers was built on the summit above the lighthouse, but the men spent much of their time at the lighthouse or fog signal building. A trip down the long staircase from the dwelling to the lighthouse could be challenging, especially on windy days. Winds of 60 miles per hour are common on the point. The highest recorded wind was 133 miles per hour.

Three to five men rotated duty at Point Reyes, standing watch in the service building at the lighthouse, cleaning and fueling the oil lamps, and when necessary working the fog signal. The beacon had a clockwork system to rotate it. A 170-pound weight was suspended below the lens and had to be wound up every two hours to keep the lens turning.

For much of its career, fog signaling dominated the work at Point Reyes. The area averages about 2,100-hours of fog annually and topped Lighthouse Service records for hours of operation of a fog signal. A fog signal building with boilers and a locomotive-type steam whistle was placed below the tower in 1870 and a 338-step staircase was built down to it. A coal chute also snaked down to the site. On one occasion, the fog persisted for 176 hours straight, requiring the crew to shovel more than 12 tons of coal into the boilers to maintain enough steam to power the fog whistle. The boilers required a great deal of water, which was not readily available on the point. A horse-drawn water wagon with a large tank mounted on it was used to fetch water from the nearest settlement at Olema. In 1915 the fog signal was changed to a gasoline-powered diaphone horn and the building housing it was moved up the precipice and next to the light tower. In 1934, it was changed to an electric foghorn.

The site was somewhat remote in its early years of service. The Lighthouse Service tender usually brought supplies, inspectors, and work crews, but keepers also had to go by foot or on horseback to Olema for food, to see a doc-tor, attend church, and to send their children to school. Conditions improved as the region's population increased in the early twentieth century. By the time the station was transferred to the Coast Guard in 1940, vehicular travel was commonplace and the station had electricity. The lighthouse was automated in 1975 when a modern optic and electric foghorns were installed. The light station then became the centerpiece of Point Reyes National Seashore.

Light station exhibits are housed in the Bear Valley Interpretive Center at Point Reyes Station. Visitors access the lighthouse and fog signal building via a 300-step staircase with rest areas. It's the same staircase keepers used to visit the tower several times a day and stand their watches.

Gone but Not Forgotten

Technological progress and changes in shipping needs have rendered a number of old California lighthouses obsolete or substantially altered. Vestiges of these bygone lights remain in new locations with sometimes curious duties.

Mile Rocks Lighthouse on the south side of the entrance to San Francisco Bay was once a handsome, four-tiered, white tower perched on a caisson. It bore a strong resemblance to a huge a wedding cake. Its upper tiers were removed in 1966 and replaced by a helicopter pad. Now only a small plastic beacon remains. The photos show the lighthouse before and after its unattractive transformation.

Lime Point Lighthouse began service in the 1880s as a fog signal station on the north side of the Golden Gate. It was lighted in 1900 with a small lens-lantern mounted on its south wall. The dwelling was torn down in the early 1960s and the remaining fog signal building is an eyesore. A modern beacon still serves vessels, though in a much diminished capacity on a metal post. The photo is circa 1930.

Oakland Harbor Light went into service in 1890 on wooden piers in the harbor. After several iterations of structures, a housetop lantern served until 1966 when it was decommissioned. The lantern went to Mark Abbott Memorial Lighthouse and the wooden lighthouse itself became a restaurant at Embarcadero Cove.

Carquinez Strait Lighthouse. Built in 1910 to mark the entrance to the Napa River, the sentinel served for half a century before deactivation. It was sold in 1955 and moved to Glen Cove Marina where it still sits today, housing the marina office. The photo, from about 1935, shows the sentinel in its heyday.

Southhampton Shoal Lighthouse stood watch on a navigational hazard in San Francisco Bay a short distance west of Berkeley. It served from 1905 until 1960 (left), until the Coast Guard removed it and placed a pole beacon on the shoal. The pretty Victoran house-tower was moved by barge to Tinsley Island to become the St. Francis Yacht Club (right).

Año Nuevo Lighthouse served first as a fog signal and later a light-house from 1872 to 1948. The station is pictured about 1920 after the beacon had been moved from a round water tower to a skeleton tower. All that remains of the once vibrant station today is the shell of its dwellings and the toppled light tower. It sits in a protected wildlife area and is off-limits to the public.

Point Arena Lighthouse   38.95N, 123.79W

FOR MORE INFORMATION
Point Arena Lighthouse Keepers
P.O. Box 11
Point Arena, CA 95468
877.725.4448
palight@mcn.org
www.mcn.org/1/palight

DIRECTIONS
From Coastal Highway 1 at
Rollerville Junction in Point
Arena, turn west and take Light-
house Road to the site.

Point Arena, or "sandy point" in Spanish, is a landmark for ships headed south into San Francisco. Its original lighthouse, a 100-foot-tall brick tower built in 1870, had a first-order fixed Fresnel lens. The quadraplex keepers' dwelling sat near the tower, and a steam whistle served in periods of fog. The fog signal building had to be replaced in 1896 after erosion threatened the original structure.

The station is located near where the San Andreas Fault runs out to sea. Repeated earthquakes, noted in the station logbook, wracked the point. Each one caused slight damage, but in 1906, the great San Francisco Earthquake destroyed the light tower and the dwelling, and damaged other buildings. A peculiar result of the quake was the appearance of a black bear that raged onto the station, threatening the families; it had to be shot.

A reinforced-concrete tower, 115 feet tall, was built the following year. A ring of concrete encircled the base to give the tower added stability. A new first-order Fresnel lens manufactured by the French com-pany Barbier, Bernard & Turenne, was installed in the new tower. It operated with a mercury float system to support and turn the heavy lens. At the same time, four new bungalows were built for the keepers.

In the 1960s the Coast Guard replaced the keepers' homes with more modern ranch-style homes. The light was automated with a modern aerobeacon in 1977. In 1984 the nonprofit Point Arena Lighthouse Keepers took over the site and converted the homes into unique vacation rentals. The 1900 fog signal building became a museum.

Major restoration of the station was done in 2008, including removal of the lens and its relocation to the museum.

The April 18, 1906 Earthquake

Point Bonita Lighthouse

Terrible earthquake occurred at 5:13 a.m. doing considerable damage to the Assts quarters shaking the gable ends out and cracking it so badly that it was with difficulty that the families were taken out without injury to their persons. The chimneys were shaken to pieces. The keepers quarters were given a terrible shaking. Our chimney shaken off at the comb of the roof and the others broken off but still stand. The doors were all jammed so the keeper had to take his family out of the kitchen window. The tanks at the [fog] signal were moved about one inch starting them to leaking but the leak was stopped. The chimney to the signal was cracked clear around about 6 feet from the bottom but it still stands. The old tower [original lighthouse built in 1855] is nearly ready to fall, being cracked.

Point Arena Lighthouse

A heavy blow first struck the tower from the south. The blow came quick and heavy, accompanied by a heavy report. The tower quivered for a few seconds, went far over to the north, came back, and then swung north again, repeating this several times. Immediately after came rapid and violent vibrations, rending the tower apart, the sections grinding and grating upon each; while the lenses, reflectors, etc., in the lantern were shaken from their settings and fell in a shower upon the iron floor.

Nov 14/06
POINT ARENA

Point Cabrillo Lighthouse   39.34N, 123.82W

FOR MORE INFORMATION
Point Cabrillo Lightkeepers Assoc.
P.O. Box 641
Mendocino, CA 95460
info@pointcabrillo.org
www.pointcabrillo.org
Cottage Rental 707.937.5033

HOURS OF OPERATION
Museum and Gift Shop open daily
10 A.M. to 4 P.M. Grounds open
dawn to dusk.

DIRECTIONS
Two miles north of Mendocino on
Coastal Highway 1, turn onto Point
Cabrillo Road at Russian Gulch.
Follow signs to the lighthouse.

Built in 1909 in response to shipwrecks and the redwood lumber trade, the Point Cabrillo Lighthouse lit a 100-mile-long, dark gap on the Mendocino Coast. The point is named for the Spanish explorer Juan Rodriguez Cabrillo, the first European to navigate the coast of California in 1542.

The 32-foot-tall wooden tower, incorporated into a dual air siren fog signal building, resembled a small country church. Its third-order flashing Fresnel lens, manufactured in Birmingham, England by Chance Brothers, was fueled by a kerosene lamp and had an unusual design with four bulls-eyes.

Inland from the lighthouse were three comfortable keepers' dwellings. A barn and a blacksmith shop were located behind the dwellings. An oil house to store the volatile kerosene was erected between the lighthouse and the homes, safely away from all other buildings in case it caught fire.

The fuel in the lens was changed to incandescent oil vapor in 1911. The lamp was electrified in 1935. In 1972 the lens was turned off and replaced by an automatic aero-marine beacon mounted on the roof of the fog signal building. The station was then boarded up and suffered considerable deterioration before the property was purchased by the California State Coastal Preserve in 1988.

With the help of the North Coast Interpretive Association, the lighthouse was restored over a period of several years. The lens and lantern were dismantled, cleaned, and repaired, and the light was reactivated inside the historic lens in 1999. One of the dwellings became a museum and the other two were opened as vacation rentals. A gift shop was set up in the fog signal building.

Sitting in a field of grass and wildflowers, Point Cabrillo Light has undergone total restoration. The wooden tower is attached to a fog signal building, which now serves as a museum. The opulent third-order lens has been refurbished and returned to service. The station has many of its original buildings and is one of the best examples of an extant working light station.

Punta Gorda Lighthouse   40.24N, 124.34W

DIRECTIONS
From Highway 1 at Petrolia, take Mattole Road to Lighthouse Road. Park at the beach and walk 3.5 miles to the lighthouse. The walk is rigorous, with several small creeks to cross. The beach is gravelly and can be impassable at high tide. On foggy days the trail is sometimes difficult to follow.

Swift currents and high winds make the Mendocino coast a dangerous place. It projects into the ocean close to the shipping lanes. This is why Spanish explorers decided to name this part of the coast Punta Gorda, or "plump point." Many vessels have perished here. The 1908 wreck of the *Columbia*, with the loss of eighty-seven lives, may have been the worst, since it spurred Congress to appropriate money for a lighthouse to mark the spot.

A light station was built at Punta Gorda in 1912 about 12 miles south of the town of Petrolia. The modest 27-foot tower consisted of an iron lantern perched on a square concrete building. Three dwellings, a fog signal house, a barn, and a work shed completed the station. Horses were a critical part of the crew, since supplies were packed in and out of the station over a difficult beach trail often awash in the tide.

During World War II, Coast Guard "beach pounders" patrolled the point keeping an eye out for enemy ships and submarines. The patrols were done on foot and horseback. After the war a rough road was built to the station to allow travel by Jeep, but the light's tenure was about to end. The lighthouse was extinguished in 1951 after only thirty-nine years of service. It was expensive to maintain, and the need for the beacon had diminished over the years.

The property was transferred to the Bureau of Land Management in 1963. Many of the buildings were razed after they were used as hangouts by beach-goers. Only the tower and oil house remain. The whereabouts of the lens is unknown. A few years ago the California Conservancy Corps painted both structures. There are no doors on either building. Visitors energetic enough to make the long hike to the site can get inside the lighthouse.

Pack animals were the mainstay of transportation early in Punta Gorda Light Station's career. Even in 1940 (bottom), horses still carried most of the supplies from the town of Petrolia. Today, Punta Gorda Light is a ghost sentinel (top), with only the shell of the tower and the oilhouse remaining.

Cape Mendocino Lighthouse   40.44N, 124.40W

DIRECTIONS

From US 101 about 2 miles north of Garberville, turn west at the sign for Shelter Cove. Drive 25 miles to Ferndale and the Humboldt County Fairgrounds, where the lighthouse now sits.

California's westernmost point is home to Cape Mendocino Lighthouse. Its name was chosen by explorer Juan Rodriguez Cabrillo in 1542 to honor the first viceroy of New Spain, Don Antonio de Mendoza. It marks an area of dangerous rocks, including Blunts Reef, which was long ago marked by a lightship.

Ships make an important course change here on the route to and from San Francisco. The coast is so dangerous even the supply ship *Shrubick*, bringing building materials for construction of the lighthouse in September 1867, hit the rocks and was damaged.

The light station was opened in December 1868 with a first-order revolving Fresnel lens. The 43-foot, sixteen-sided tower was constructed of iron plates and was perched 422 feet above the ocean. Though its beacon could be seen for about 28 miles in good weather, the loom of the light (glow over the horizon) often stretched farther. A dwelling was situated behind the tower but had to be rebuilt after an 1870 earthquake ruined it.

The station experienced many severe storms over the years with damage to the keepers' dwellings, but the iron tower stood firm. In one storm, the lighthouse inspector from San Francisco arrived on board the tender *Manzanita* with pay for the keepers. His small launch capsized in the waves on the way to shore, and the weight of gold coins in his pockets pulled him under. He and two others in the launch drowned.

In 1948 after a modern beacon replaced the Fresnel lens, the lens was taken to nearby Ferndale and displayed in a replica tower. The lighthouse itself was extinguished in 1951, and the beacon was placed on a pole near the defunct lighthouse. Earthquake damage in 1992, along with vandalism, nearly spelled the end for the old tower. But in 1998 the lighthouse was dismantled and transported by helicopter to Mel Coombs Park for restoration. It now serves as an exhibit on the Shelter Harbor shorefront. The tower is not open but the grounds around it are.

A view of the lighthouse circa 1940 (above) shows drapes drawn around the lens to protect it from the harmful effects of sunlight, which could discolor the glass and dry out the putty holding the prisms and lens panels in place. The solid fence behind the lighthouse probably protected it from heavy winds. The tower was dismantled and taken to a park in Shelter Harbor in 1998. Its replacement (below) is a less attractive but more functional pole with a double, rotating aero-marine beacon.

Table Bluff Lighthouse   40.69N, 124.27W

DIRECTIONS

From US 101 in Eureka, take SR 225 to Woodley Island. Follow signs to the marina and the lighthouse, standing in the marina parking area.

A guide for Humboldt Bay, the lighthouse was built in 1892 to replace the aging, cottage-style Humboldt Bay Light on North Spit, which was plagued by erosion and earthquakes. The new tower, seated on a plateau 165 feet above the sea and four miles south of the entrance to Humboldt Bay, was a duplicate of the Victorian sentinels at Ballast Point, Point Fermin, and Point San Luis. The old Humboldt Bay Light's fixed fourth-order lens was transferred to the new tower.

The station also had an assistant keepers' duplex and a fog signal, plus an oil house and a shop. Keepers had a large garden, a chicken coop, and space to graze a cow. The lighthouse served as a lookout post and radio station during World War II. Barracks were built for additional Coast Guard staff whose job was to stand watches and patrol the beach looking for enemy activity.

The lighthouse was occupied by lightkeepers until after the war. The residence attached to the base of the lighthouse was torn down by the Coast Guard; only the square tower remained. It was automated in 1953. The classical Fresnel lens was removed and sent to Old Point Loma Lighthouse in San Diego for display. A modern aerobeacon replaced the lens. The fog signal was discontinued at this time as well.

A church group occupied the buildings for a time, then in 1975 the lighthouse was discontinued and the site was closed. It stood vacant and vandalized for several years. Local residents removed the upper half of the tower in 1987 and took it to Woodley Island Marina for display. The original lens was brought from San Diego and now is exhibited on Woodley Island at Humboldt Bay Maritime Museum on Second Street. The tower is closed to visitors but the grounds are accessible.

Lovely Table Bluff Lighthouse was a Carpenter Gothic design with a tower incorporated into the dwelling. The lighthouse was built to replace the Humboldt Bay Light, which was situated too near the water and was an unstable structure. These images from about 1945 show the radio antennas, one behind the lighthouse (bottom) and the other to the right of the fog signal building (top). A large barracks, seen on the right (top), was built for the beach patrols that occupied the station during World War II.

Trinidad Head Lighthouse   41.05N, 124.15W

DIRECTIONS

The light station can be seen in the distance from various spots along US 101 south of Trinidad. The original lens and bell along with a replica of the lighthouse are located at the foot of Trinity Street on the waterfront in the town of Trinidad. The lighthouse on the headland is closed to the public but energetic hikers can visit the site via a road beyond Edwards Street in Trinidad that travels past the Coast Guard station and along the headland cliffs.

Northern California's Trinidad Head curls west and then south to enclose Trinidad Bay. The headland was a hazard to ships entering the busy lumber port at Trinidad and the ideal spot for a lighthouse. The sentinel helped ships negotiate the sharp turn into the bay and closed the dangerous dark gap between Crescent City and Humboldt Bay.

In order to construct the lighthouse, a dirt road had to be built from Trinidad to the southern point of Trinidad Head—no easy task considering the precipitous cliffs along the headland. Teams of horses brought building materials, and a small brick lighthouse was placed in service in 1871. It was perched on a niche in the headland 175 feet above sea. A spacious, two-story keeper's house was erected about 150 feet behind the lighthouse. A cistern stored rainwater. Completing the station was a white picket fence along the front of the house and the trail leading to the lighthouse.

In 1898 a fog signal was added to the station, a two-ton bell whose percussive bongs loosened rocks on the cliff and sent them plummeting into the sea. The fogbell was hung in a belfry beside a bell-striker house about 50 feet below the dwelling and was run by a clockwork system with weights suspended down the cliff. In foggy weather the keeper wound up the weights every few hours to keep the bell-striker operating. The cable holding the weights snapped one windy day, and they fell into the sea. To resolve the issue, an enclosed weight

shaft was built to protect a set of new weights.

The site was plagued by wind, storms, and fog. During a strong storm in December 1914, lightkeeper Fred Harrington observed waves washing over 93-foot-high Pilot Rock south of the light station. As he worked in the lantern room, a large wave approached the shore, scaled the cliff, and struck the lighthouse. The tower shuddered, and the lens stopped rotating. It took the keeper a half-hour to restart it. The storm continued for several days. Harrington, a longtime veteran of lightkeeping, noted it was the most severe storm he had ever experienced.

When the station was electrified in 1942 the fogbell was replaced by an electric horn. In 1947, the fourth-order Fresnel lens was removed and a small, modern drum lens was installed. The old lens and bell were put on display on the waterfront in the town of Trinidad. The keeper's house eventually was torn down, and a triplex was built for Coast Guard personnel. The station was automated in the 1970s. The lighthouse and bell house are the only buildings remaining on the site.

Battery Point Lighthouse   41.74N, 124.20W

FOR MORE INFORMATION
Del Norte Historical Society
577 H Street
Crescent City, CA 95531
www.delnortehistory.org

HOURS OF OPERATION
Open April through September,
tide permitting. For tours of the
lighthouse during these months call
707.464.3089

DIRECTIONS
From US 101 in Crescent City, turn
west on Front Street, then south on
A Street to a parking area. Take the
short walk to the lighthouse at low
tide. Consult tide tables to prevent
being marooned on the island as
the tide rises.

A small islet about 200 yards offshore of Crescent City is the site of the 1856 Battery Point Lighthouse, one of the first sentinels established on the West Coast. The islet takes its name from three cannons that were mounted on it following their salvage from a shipwreck.

The 45-foot brick light tower was incorporated into a small keeper's cottage. The original beacon was a fourth-order flashing Fresnel lens. It served the small port of Crescent City, an entry point to the gold fields and passes of interior Northern California and Oregon.

Because the islet was separated from the mainland by a tidal channel, keepers had to time their trips ashore in accordance with low tide. The offshore location also made the site vulnerable to storm waves, which occasionally dashed up and hit the lighthouse. One such storm broke several windows on the lantern.

The lighthouse was automated in 1953 and extinguished altogether in 1965 when a breakwater light took over its duties. In 1982 the Coast Guard gave the lighthouse to the Del Norte Historical Society, which restored and relighted it as a private aid to navigation. Live-in caretakers open the lighthouse for tours and operate a small gift shop. Visitors must be mindful of the tide. During the summer season a sign on the mainland posts low tide hours.

Battery Point Light's small islet was sometimes washed by waves in storms at high tide. The tide controlled access to the islet. At low tide (top) the keepers could traverse the rocky seabed to shore. High tide (bottom) covered the small isthmus and cut off the islet from the mainland. The station's water tower is visible in both images, circa 1940.

St. George Reef Lighthouse 41.83N, 124.37W

FOR MORE INFORMATION
St. George Reef Lighthouse
Preservation Society
P.O. Box 577
Crescent City, CA 95531
707.464.8299
tours@stgeorgereeflighthouse.us
www.stgeorgereeflighthouse.us

The most expensive light-house in the United States, St. George Reef Light, went into service in 1892 to mark dangerous rocks nine miles off the coast. Capt. George Vancouver named the reef the Dragon Rocks in the 1790s, but settlers in the area preferred the name St. George, for a point of land facing the sea and the rocks.

St. George Reef caused numerous shipwrecks in the early years of West Coast exploration and settlement. The worst was the 1865 wreck of the side-wheeler *Brother Jonathan*, which claimed 225 lives. Public outcry over the loss forced Congress to consider a lighthouse for the reef, but funding did not become available for more than twenty years because of the enormous Civil War debt.

Appropriations totaling $150,000—a princely sum in 1883—allowed construction of a lighthouse to begin. But much more money was needed before the project was complete. The off-shore stone tower took almost ten years to construct at a total cost of $704,000. The price tag included its first-order lens, which went into service on October 20, 1892 flashing red and white.

Because of the difficulties of living on a rock at sea, only men were permitted to live on the remote light tower. Storms and isolation made their lives difficult. A crew of five keepers rotated duty three months at the station and two months off. By far the most dangerous part of the work was getting on and off the tower, lifted by derrick in a small boat. In 1951 several Coast Guard keepers were killed while being transferred to the lighthouse by this means. In 1975 their work ended when a large lighted navigation buoy was anchored west of the lighthouse.

St. George Reef Light was decommissioned. Its lens was removed and put on display in the Del Norte Country Historical Society Museum. The tower stood dark and forlorn for a number of years until the nonprofit St. George Reef Preservation Society began restoration of the tower in 1996. The entire iron lantern was removed and brought ashore for repairs. In 2002 the lantern was reset, and the light was put back in the tower with a modern optic. It operates today as a private aid to navigation.

On clear days, the lighthouse can be seen from beaches near Crescent City. St. George Reef Preservation Society occasionally offers helicopter trips to the lighthouse.

A Billy Pugh-like net, or transfer basket, provided access from a pulling boat at the landing to the concrete platform at the base of the lighthouse. It was often a wild ride in the wind and waves.

St. George Reef as seen by helicopter, 2006

*Stellar sea lions can be seen lounging on the rocks
in front of the old concrete landing.*

Fog Sounds

Fog signaling work was as important at lighthouses as keeping the light. When the air became thick and the light failed to shine the necessary distance, sound became the seaman's guide. Though a boon for ships, it meant hours of hard work and incessant noise for the lighthouse families.

Fog plagued the entire West Coast, but Northern California and the Pacific Northwest were socked-in as much as a quarter of the year. San Francisco is renowned for its fog. A symphony of bongs, chimes, honks, and roars sing to the seaman when the murk rolls into the bay. Point Reyes Light, a few miles north of the city, often held the national fog record. Its horns blared roughly three days out of five. Many of Puget Sound's sentinels started their careers as fog signal stations and later segued into light stations. Alaskan lighthouses dealt with ice fogs and what lightkeepers called "sea smoke," a thick fog that not only obscured the light but also played devious tricks with sound signals.

A variety of devices and methods were tested by the Lighthouse Service to penetrate the fog. The first keeper at Old Point Loma Lighthouse in San Diego fired his shotgun at regular intervals when fog descended on the promontory.

A cannon set up at San Francisco's Point Bonita Lighthouse in the 1850s was fired every half hour in poor visibility. But the cost for shot was high and the sound carried poorly over the sea. Also, it was difficult to find a keeper willing to do the work. One man, a retired Army sergeant the Lighthouse Service felt was well-equipped to deal with the interminable fog and the cantankerous cannon, resigned after only a few days. His primary complaints

were exhaustion and lack of sleep. In the war against Golden Gate fog, the fog won.

Bells came into use in 1820 for fog signaling. These were rung by hand, taking up much of the keepers' time and energy. By about 1860 most had automatic bell strikers that operated with clockworks; keepers only had to wind up the weights of the system to keep gears turning and the bells bonging. They were the mainstay of fog signaling at many West Coast lighthouses. The sound carried well over the water but also caused vibrations that sometimes loosened paint from the walls and jiggled cups in the cupboard, not to mention disturbing sleep. The huge bell at Ediz Hook Lighthouse in Port Angeles, Washington set all the metal parts of the light station sympathetically humming.

Steam-powered fog signals also were in use by the mid-nineteenth century, including whistles, horns, and sirens mounted on steam boilers. The familiar two-tone honk of the diaphone horn came along in the 1870s, and the multi-toned diaphragm horn arrived a decade later. For the keepers, these were labor-intensive mechanisms. The men spent hours shoveling coal into boilers and coddling their delicate settings. Electricity eventually relieved much of this work.

Along the way, myriad peculiar inventions came and went. A wave-actuated fog signal was installed at Farallon Light off San Francisco. It used the rush of waves through a blowhole to produce a burst of air that caused a locomotive whistle to scream. The device was unsuccessful, though, since the whistle sounded irregularly and depended on choppy seas to work. Fog usually rolls in when seas are calm. In a frustrating reverse of function, the whistle was silent on murky days and shrieked relentlessly when the wind picked up and seas were rough.

Colorful comments about fog signals were popular entries in lightkeepers' logbooks and diaries. At Point Reyes Light in California it was noted that the lighthouse children used the coal chute as a sliding board, though the fun was dangerous and resulted in a broken leg on one occasion. A Point Reyes mother glibly wrote that her baby's first words were not the traditional "ma-ma" or "da-da," but a roaring "be-ooohhh!" In foggy Washington, Cape

Flattery's lightkeepers learned to pause in their conversations when the fog signal sounded, and they often maintained the odd habit long after retirement. A few miles down the coast at Destruction Island Lighthouse, a lightkeeper's bull mistook the station's new foghorn for a rival bull and attacked it.

No matter the sound, there was always commentary. People ashore either loved or hated the lighthouse fog signals. Most considered the sounds a welcome lullaby from the sea, while a few objected to the near-constant cacophony. Some didn't understand fog signaling at all. In the 1880s, a Salish Indian observed government workers building a fog signal in Puget Sound, all the time wondering how it would work. When the horn roared to life, he pronounced it useless: "Horn go boo! boo! all the time, but fog come in anyway."

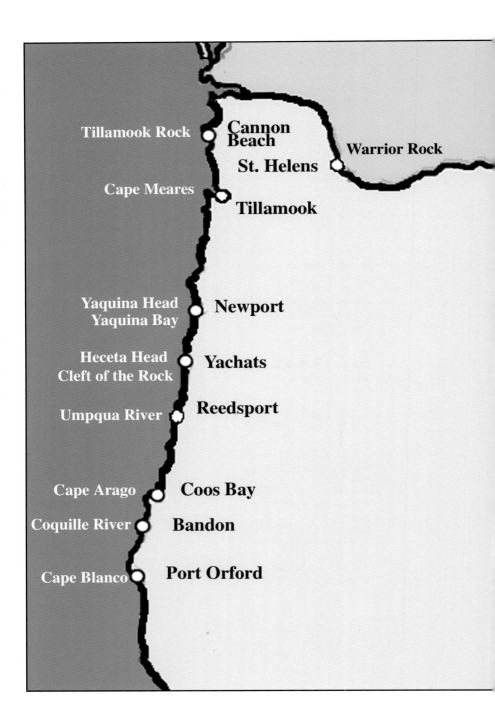

Tillamook Rock

Cannon
Beach

Warrior Rock

St. Helens

Cape Meares

Tillamook

Yaquina Head
Yaquina Bay

Newport

Heceta Head
Cleft of the Rock

Yachats

Umpqua River

Reedsport

Cape Arago

Coos Bay

Coquille River

Bandon

Cape Blanco

Port Orford

Lighthouses of Oregon

Explorers and settlers encountered fewer perils along the Oregon coast than in other parts of the Pacific. Though Oregon was dotted with capes and headlands and pounded by winter storms, only one major navigational obstacle faced mariners between Northern California and the Columbia River—the critical turning point at Cape Blanco.

But surprisingly, it was not the first place along the Oregon Coast to be lighted. While nine lighthouses were planned for California, and five for what would someday become the state of Washington, Congress felt Oregon needed only one lighthouse. Funds were precious in the 1850s, and Oregon lacked the large ports of California and the major waterways of Washington. As a result, it was left out of the lighthouse boom.

The site chosen for Oregon's first lighthouse was the Umpqua River, named for the natives of the coast. A burgeoning lumber trade and discovery of gold in southwest Oregon Territory spurred the growth of a settlement at the river mouth. The lighthouse was constructed in 1857, but it lasted only four years. In the spring of 1861, a heavy snowpack in the mountains melted and flooded the Umpqua River, washing away the lighthouse. It was several years before it would be rebuilt.

Strapped for funding by the Civil War, Congress did little to improve West Coast lighthouses until after 1865. By then, other ports had gained importance. Cape Arago Light was built in 1866 on an islet off the entrance to the busy lumber port of Coos Bay. In 1870, Cape Blanco, the most dangerous headland along the coast and the major reckoning point for ships, was lighted.

As the nation pulled out of debt from the Civil War, a flurry of lighthouse construction followed. The dramatic, sea-swept sentinel on Tillamook Rock, on a stump of basalt a mile off Cannon

Beach, flashed on in 1881 as an aid to ships headed in and out of the Columbia River. It quickly earned a reputation as the worst place to work on the West Coast. Umpqua River Lighthouse was rebuilt in 1894. That same year, stunning Heceta Head Light went into service and was immediately dubbed the most beautiful lighthouse on the West Coast. Six more Oregon lighthouses were in operation by 1900.

As Oregon moved into the twentieth century, its lighthouse construction slowed. Desdemona Sands Light, built in 1902 on a mudflat in the Columbia River, was the last sentinel built in the state. Discontinued in 1934, it washed away piece by piece as the river reshaped its course. The fabulous Fresnel lens from the lighthouse ended up in a private home. It was later found by a historian from Mukilteo, Washington and placed on display in Mukilteo Lighthouse.

By the late 1980s all Oregon lighthouses had been automated. Slowly, they were leased or given to private groups or government agencies to ensure their care. Seven of the sentinels are now open to the public. The Oregon Chapter of the U.S. Lighthouse Society, formed in the 1990s, serves as a clearinghouse for information on the state's lighthouses. Contact the group at Oregon Chapter, c/o U. S. Lighthouse Society, 9005 Point No Point Road, Hansville, WA 98340, 415.362.7255.

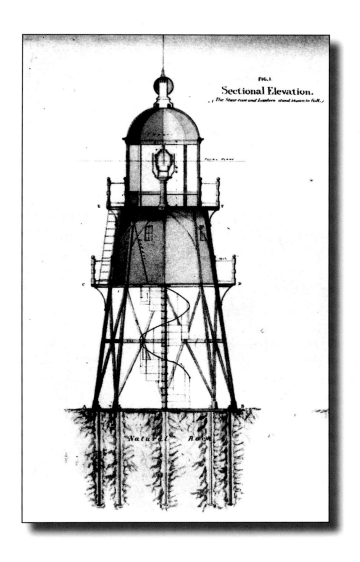

FIG.1.

Sectional Elevation.
(The Stair-case and Lantern stand shown in full.)

An 1866 U.S. Lighthouse Board drawing of Cape Arago's first lighthouse—originally called Cape Gregory—shows a peculiar but inexpensive design. The bottom half of the octagonal iron tower was an open framework of piles driven into the bedrock of the island, while the top half of the tower was enclosed. The entire structure was fabricated at a foundry and then shipped to the site in pieces, where it was quickly assembled.

Cape Blanco Light Station   42.83N, 124.56W

FOR MORE INFORMATION
Cape Blanco Heritage Society
P.O. Box 1132
Port Orford, OR 97465
541.332.0521
www.capeblancoheritagesociety.com

HOURS OF OPERATION
Tuesday through Sunday, 10
A.M. to 3:30 P.M.

DIRECTIONS
From US 101 north of Port
Orford, drive west on Cape
Blanco Highway for about
five miles.

Cape Blanco, or "white cape," is the westernmost point in Oregon. The proprietor of a hotel in the town of Port Orford set up the first beacon here by hanging a lantern from his establishment. The lighthouse that today marks this critical turning point for ships was built in 1870. The cliffs are steep here and rise some 200 feet above the sea. The point was once densely forested, but many of the trees were removed so the beacon would not be obstructed. It was lighted a few days before Christmas, a symbolic event that delighted local citizens.

Bricks for the 59-foot tower were made on site, while the remainder of the construction materials were landed on the beach below the bluff and moved to the top by horses and wagons. The huge first-order lens, packed in crates and straw, also was carted to the site. Complementing the conical tower was a duplex for the keepers. Another residence was built in 1890.

The lighthouse was automated in the 1980s, when it became part of Cape Blanco State Park. A few years later, the vacant station was broken into and part of the lens was shattered with a hammer. Hardin Optical of Bandon, Oregon

repaired the beautiful optic at a cost of $80,000. The entire station was refurbished by the Bureau of Land Management in 2003, including major repairs to the tower. The Cape Blanco Heritage Society opens the station for tours in summer. It is the oldest original lighthouse in Oregon.

A light veil of fog settled over the 59-foot Cape Blanco Lighthouse on a summer morning in 1985. A few years later vandals damaged the lighthouse. It has since been restored and is in the care of the Bureau of Land Management.

Coquille River Lighthouse   43.12N, 124.42W

FOR MORE INFORMATION
541.347.3501
www.oregonstateparks.org/
park_71.php

HOURS OF OPERATION
Lighthouse hours vary
throughout the year. Call
Bullard Beach State Park at
541.347.3501 for schedule.

DIRECTIONS
From the west side of Highway 101 north of Bandon,
enter Bullards Beach State
Park and follow signs to the
lighthouse.

Named for the Coquille tribe, the lighthouse has stood watch over the north jetty of the Coquille River for more than a century. The river connected inland timber operations with the Pacific Ocean, but a dangerous bar at the river mouth caused mayhem for ships headed in and out of the little port of Bandon. In 1880 a jetty was built to slow the buildup of sand and the tidal current.

A year later the lighthouse was authorized by Congress, but a lengthy period followed while land was secured and arrangements were made for construction. The 40-foot stone tower with an adjoining octagonal fog signal building was completed in 1896 on the north side of the river entrance opposite the jetty. It held a fourth-order Fresnel lens. A plank walkway led to the duplex dwelling. Behind the house was a mule barn and chicken coop.

The light station served until 1939 when the Coast Guard installed an automatic light at the end of the jetty. All buildings except the abandoned sentinel were torn down. The lighthouse was vandalized repeatedly and deteriorated badly until 1976, when Oregon State Parks adopted it. It was restored and re-lighted in 1991 as a private navigational aid. It sits inside Bullards Beach State Park amid sand dunes and sea oats. There is camping nearby.

1375. Lighthouse No 5 on the Oregon Coast.

An old postcard captured Coquille River Lighthouse in its prime, circa 1900. The 40-foot stone tower adjoined the fog signal building. A fog trumpet, run by compressed air, faced the river entrance. To the left was a wooden bridge that led from the lighthouse over the rocks to a plank walkway that traversed the sand to the keepers' dwellings.

Floating Lighthouses

In some shipping lanes, dangers existed offshore that could not be marked by lighthouses, which need a foundation of some sort.

In their place, lightships served. These floating lighthouses—a combination of ship and lighthouse—were anchored at perilous points in the sea-lanes where shallows, rocks, and shoals surreptitiously languished just beneath the surface. With a go-nowhere mission and a small crew to tend the light and fog signal, the lightship's warning to other vessels was a simple "steer clear of me!"

The first patented lightship design was the *Nore*, anchored in England's Thames River estuary in 1731. She was a small wooden boat with an oil lamp hung from a single mast. Less than a century later, the first lightships appeared in the United States at Willoughby Spit, Virginia and Northeast Pass, Louisiana. They were small boats with single lighted masts anchored over or near hazards. A lamplighter rowed out to each vessel nightly to kindle the beacon and returned at dawn to extinguish it.

In the 1840s, revenue cutters were refitted as lightships and permanent crews were enlisted. By the 1860s, two sizes of lightships were in use. Small vessels weighed 100 tons or less; larger lightships were as heavy as 300 tons. "Inside" lightships served in rivers, bays, and sounds. "Outside" lightships were anchored off coastlines, sometimes miles at sea.

Lightship duty was tedious and sometimes dangerous. Crews of six to twelve men—women never served on lightships—who sometimes called themselves "fish," lived on board in crowded quarters and worked long hours without any change in scenery. Storms could be terrifying. Fogbells and horns deprived crew members of sleep. Seasickness affected many, since lightships

rolled almost constantly. Like all seamen, the crews missed their families during the long weeks of duty at sea.

The signature of a lightship was its light cage or light basket, which the men tended daily. Most vessels had two masts and two baskets, mounted near the top of each mast. Gimbaled oil lamps in the baskets remained level as the ship rolled. These were filled on deck, then hoisted up the masts on their little pulley systems. Later, gas and electric lights with small lenses provided increased brilliance.

The dangers of lightship duty and the expense of operating lightships encouraged the development of other technologies to mark offshore perils. By 1987, all lightships in the United States were retired. Those on the West Coast were replaced by large navigation buoys—behemoth floating light stations with beacons, sound, and radio signals that ran on their own and reported all functions to a monitoring center ashore.

Three defunct West Coast lightships now sit in museums. The *Overfalls* lightship that once served Delaware is now owned by the U.S. Lighthouse Society and is berthed in Oakland, California and open for tours. The Columbia River Maritime Museum at Astoria, Oregon displays the last of the Columbia River's lightships, while Northwest Seaport in Seattle owns one of the Swift-sure relief vessels. The last Umatilla lightship is moored in Ketchikan, Alaska and is used as a training ship. The Salish word *umatilla*, fittingly, means "water rippling over sand," the ideal place for a lightship to anchor.

"Umatilla Reef Lightship"
(in heavy weather) off sea-coast of Oregon U.S.A.
(from a photograph).

Lightships wore the names of the stations where they anchored and had a numbering system so they could be easily identified. Later, all of them were painted red. On the West Coast they served at five outside locations—Umatilla Reef, Swiftsure Bank, and the Columbia River Bar in Washington, and Blunts Reef and San Francisco in California. Relief lightships were assigned to provide substitute duty when a regular lightship had to be towed to port for maintenance or repairs.

Lightships were designed to remain in one spot. Bulky, flattened hulls with bilge keels reduced rolling in heavy seas, while huge mushroom-shaped anchors held the vessels in position, digging firmly into the seabed. Heavy storms sometimes dragged the anchor or parted its chain, setting a lightship adrift. With little or no motive power, she became as dangerous as a derelict ship.

The Columbia River Lightship No. 50 was torn from her station during a storm in November 1899. She broke anchor, drifted, and went aground on Cape Disappointment. The government gave her up for lost, but a house-moving company in Portland, Oregon used teams of horses to hoist her onto a makeshift railway and move her a mile overland to Bakers Bay, where she was refloated and placed back in service.

Cape Arago Lighthouse 43.34N, 124.375W

DIRECTIONS
The lighthouse is located on tribal land and currently is not open to the public. It is visible from a turnout in Cape Arago State Park.

The busy port of Coos Bay got its first lighthouse in 1866. It was an octagonal iron tower perched on a platform supported by stilts. The site was Cape Gregory situated a few miles south of the bay. (It was later named Cape Arago.) An octagonal iron tower with the top enclosed and the bottom an open framework, held a fourth-order Fresnel lens. The lighthouse stood on tiny Chief's Island a few hundred feet offshore and was accessed by boat. A plank walkway ran between the lighthouse and the dwelling. The Coos tribe had once used the island as a burial ground.

Getting to shore was a bane for the keepers during the early years at the lighthouse. A footbridge was built to the islet in 1876 but nature's winter fury made short work of it, and within a few years the keepers were again using a boat to reach the mainland. In 1891 a 400-foot tramway with a cable car was built between the shore and the light station. It proved too dangerous, almost killing the keeper and his daughter and injuring the keeper's legs so severely they had to be amputated. It was shut down. Finally in 1898, a more substantial wooden bridge was built. It survives today and adds to the picturesque milieu of the light station.

That same year a fog trumpet was added to the station and a second dwelling was built to accommodate the extra keeper needed to tend the fog signal. By 1896 the tower had been strengthened with a sheath of bricks and stucco. But its service was soon to end, hastened by erosion.

A new cottage-style wooden lighthouse was constructed in 1909. It lasted until 1934 when erosion struck again, damaging the foundation beyond repair. It was moved out of harm's way and became an office building for the keepers. The original octagonal sentinel was torn down.

The third and present concrete lighthouse was built in 1934 and automated in 1966. Its classical Fresnel lens was removed in 1993 and replaced by an aerobeacon that operated until deactivation of the light station in 2006. The Fresnel lens is displayed at the Coast Guard Air Station in North Bend. The original dwelling was razed in 1957, and a few years later the 1909 lighthouse was torn down. All that remains of the once-vibrant light station at Cape Arago is the 1934 lighthouse. The footbridge was removed in 2011.

Today the island and lighthouse belong to the Confederated Tribes of the Coos. They are working to preserve and historically interpret the island and the lighthouse and make them available to visitors.

Umpqua River Light Station   43.66N, 124.198W

FOR MORE INFORMATION
Winchester Bay Merchants Association, Inc.
P. O. Box 1143
Winchester Bay, Oregon 97467
www.umpqualighthouse.org

HOURS OF OPERATION
May through October, 10 A.M. to 4 P.M. Winter tours are by appointment; call 541.271.4631.

DIRECTIONS
From Highway 101 six miles south of Reedsport, turn west into Umpqua State Park and follow signs to the lighthouse.

Established in 1857, this first lighthouse in Oregon went into service at the entrance to the Umpqua River on the south shore of Winchester Bay, where it aided vessels carrying passengers and supplies to gold fields in the interior. The river and the lighthouse were named for the Umpqua tribe of the area. The huge sand dunes south of the area were formed by the sediment-laden river, which continually changed the outline of this section of coast.

The cottage-style sentinel, with a 92-foot tower rising from its roof, was similar to the original lighthouse at New Dungeness, Washington. A third-order lens beamed 15 miles over the bay and river. The lighthouse lasted only a few years before river floods and erosion ruined it. The sentinel was abandoned in 1864. A buoy was placed in the river estuary to guide ships until a new lighthouse could be built. But it took thirty years for funds to be approved.

Umpqua Light.

The second and current lighthouse was built 165 feet above the river entrance to protect it from floods. Lighted in 1894, the 65-foot tower was crowned by an opulent ruby-panel Fresnel lens that flashed red and white. The optic was manufactured in Paris in 1890 by lens-makers Barbier & Cie. A service room adjoined the base of the lighthouse. Two homes for the keepers, a barn, and an oil house completed the station. The light station was one of few on the West Coast without a fog signal.

Today the lighthouse and grounds are maintained by the Douglas County Parks Department and are part of Umpqua River State Park. Coast Guard bungalows have replaced the Victorian keeper's dwellings. The tower, which is still active with its beautiful first-order lens, is open to visitors. There is a museum and gift shop near the lighthouse, as well as a campground.

Visitors on the Wing

Many Pacific Coast lighthouses stand in bird sanctuaries and rookeries, on wildlife refuges, and along the great avian migration routes. This is a bittersweet circumstance, for while birds are an interesting and welcome part of the lighthouse environment, they can cause problems.

Lighthouses are favorite resting spots for birds. Birds land on the towers and foul the railings, windows, decks, and roofs. Lightkeepers spent a good portion of their time cleaning bird droppings from the lantern and other surfaces. Where water was collected from rooftops and piped into cisterns for use by the lighthouse keepers, constant cleaning was required.

"When storm clouds were sighted, the whole family hauled out the buckets and soap," recalled the grandson of a New Dungeness Light Station keeper in Washington. The bird mess was hastily scrubbed away from the catchment area to prepare for the clean rainwater that would fill the cistern.

Birds find ample spots for nesting at light stations, sometimes in the worst places. In the days of oil lamps, small bird nests had to be cleared regularly from the ventilator in the cupola at Point Conception Lighthouse in California. A plugged ventilator interfered with the proper burning of the lamps.

Farther up the coast at East Brother Island Light Station near San Francisco, nesting in the foghorns was a problem. The horns were tested every autumn after a long summer of no fog. Birds and their nests would be blown out of the horns by the immense concussion of sound. Sometimes gulls crawled into the horns and died, creating a horrendous smell. The only way to dislodge them was to fire up the boiler and let the horns roar.

Lured by the light in a tall tower, or confused by it, birds often slam into lighthouses at night. Lightkeepers' logbooks are rife with such events. James Gibbs, who served on Tillamook Rock Lighthouse in 1945, wrote, "Sometimes they flew directly into the powerful beam in the calmest weather, but more frequently it was the stress of storms that claimed the greatest number. It is generally believed that they are blinded but…for no apparent reason they will dive at the light as if drawn by a magnet, attacking like a dive-bomber and shattering themselves against the panes of glass."

Some keepers considered the birds a perk. During World War I, when food rationing took place, a flock of ducks slammed into Yaquina Head Lighthouse. There was no damage to the tower, but for several days afterward, keeper Fred Booth and his family feasted on roast duck, duck pot pie, and duck soup.

Large birds could cause considerable damage if they collided with the lantern. In 1880 a flock of geese flew into the windows of Piedras Blancas Lighthouse in California. They shattered the lantern panes and chipped some prisms on the first-order lens. The cost for repairs ran several hundred dollars.

Bird hunting was routine for many lightkeepers and provided food at isolated stations where delivery of provisions could be held up by storms and heavy seas. Wild bird eggs comprised a great part of the lighthouse diet. Farallon Island Lighthouse off San Francisco has a huge seabird rookery surrounding it. Its light-keepers sometimes complained about the noise and smell of the birds but were thankful for the eggs. One man even sold seabird eggs to San Francisco bakeries to earn a second income. His enterprise angered the city's egg hunters, who felt the keeper had an unfair advantage over them, living so close to the rookery. "Egg Wars" erupted, and the government intervened to cool down tempers.

In spite of the trouble birds caused, bird watching was a popular pastime for most lightkeepers. They kept lists of the kinds of birds they sighted, drew pictures of them, and sometimes conducted bird counts or collected specimens for scientists. Laura Hecox, keeper of Santa Cruz Lighthouse from 1881 to 1917, was an amateur zoologist who started a small museum of marine life at her home. It included a variety of local birds. A lightkeeper at Washington's Slip Point Lighthouse did taxidermy in his free time. Years after the lighthouse was decommissioned, his stuffed birds were discovered in the attic of the abandoned keeper's dwelling.

There were lonesome days too, when birds were beloved companions for lightkeepers. The men at Tillamook Rock Lighthouse were charmed by the swallows living in the nooks and crannies near the tower. Their soft chatter and the tending of their young brightened an otherwise gray existence for the keepers. "The young swallow had her first fly today," one man wrote in the log. The men kept watch as she matured, nested, and raised her own babies. With no women allowed on this offshore Tillamook Light, this tiny female's activities were cherished reminders of their loved ones ashore.

Cleft of the Rock Lighthouse   44.29N, 124.11W

This private lighthouse was built in 1976 by maritime author James Gibbs. The quaint wooden tower adjoins his beach home on a "cleft of rock" 100 feet above tiny Deception Bay at Cape Perpetua. The white

DIRECTIONS
The lighthouse is private and not accessible to the public. It can be seen from a hairpin turn on Highway 101 a few miles south of the small town Yachats.

and red flashing light, visible for 20 miles, was made an official Coast Guard beacon in 1979. The name of the lighthouse is from a Christian hymn.

Gibbs, a Coast Guard lightkeeper at Tillamook Lighthouse from 1945 to 1946 and a respected maritime author, built Cleft of the Rock Lighthouse using blueprints from the now-obsolete Fiddle Reef Lighthouse near Victoria, British Columbia. The tower's beacon is a retired optic from Solander Lighthouse off Vancouver Island's western shore.

The square-truncated wooden sentinel at Cleft of the Rock imitates Canadian-style lighthouses and has the beacon from a defunct British Columbia lighthouse.

Heceta Head Lighthouse   44.137N, 124.127W

FOR MORE INFORMATION
Heceta Head B&B
P.O. Box 250
Yachats, OR 97498
keepers@hecetalighthouse.
com
www.hecetalighthouse.com
www.oregonstateparks.org/
park_124.php

HOURS OF OPERATION
Hours vary throughout the
year. Contact www.heceta-
lighthouse.com for tour dates
and times.

DIRECTIONS
From Highway 101 thirteen
miles north of Florence, turn
west into the parking area
at Heceta Head State Scenic
Viewpoint and follow the
marked trail to the light station.

The 56-foot lighthouse stands on a magnificent headland north of Florence at the entrance to Cape Creek. The tower perches in a clearing about a quarter of the way up the face of 1,000-foot-high Heceta Head, named for Spanish explorer Don Bruno Heceta. It has served shipping since 1894 and is one of the most photographed lighthouses in the nation.

Building the lighthouse was no easy task, since the area was wilderness at the time, and no roads led to the point. Lighthouse historian Kraig Anderson notes: "Construction of the lighthouse began in 1892. Lumber came from local mills, the masonry and cement came from San Francisco, and rock used in the base of the tower was quarried from the Clackamas River near Oregon City. Laborers were paid $2 a day and worked an average of ten hours a day. The highest paid carpenter received $4 a day."

Materials were landed in the cove below the site, and teams of horses hauled everything to the headland.

The lighthouse had an adjoining service room and a detached oil house. The tower's first-order lens was manufactured by Chance Brothers of Birmingham, England. It contained 640 polished prisms in eight bulls-eye

panels. A single dwelling, a duplex, and a barn were constructed several hundred yards east of the lighthouse.

The light was electrified in 1934 and automated in 1963. The station then became part of the Siuslaw National Forest. In 2000 the Coast Guard repaired the Fresnel lens, which had begun to lean perilously. A temporary light served until the lens was ceremoniously relighted on March 1, 2001. Shining 21 miles at sea, it is the most powerful light on the Oregon Coast.

Only one of the two Queen Anne-style keepers' residences remains. It has been converted to a bed and breakfast inn. The first floor has an interpretive center. A small gift shop is located in the old garage and is open Memorial Day through Labor Day from 11 A.M. to 5 P.M.

Yaquina Bay Lighthouse   44.62N, 124.06W

FOR MORE INFORMATION
Friends of Yaquina Light-
houses
750 Lighthouse Drive, #7
Newport, OR 97355
541. 574.3100
www.yaquinalights.org

HOURS OF OPERATION
Open daily except Christmas,
New Year's, and Thanksgiv-
ing. Memorial Day to Labor
Day hours are daily 11 A.M. to
5 P.M. Off-season, open daily
from 12 P.M. to 4 P.M.

DIRECTIONS
From Highway 101 in New-
port, follow signs for Yaquina
Bay State Park and Historic
Lighthouse. The lighthouse
is located at the west end of
Elisabeth Street.

A wooden cottage-style lighthouse was built on a hill overlooking Yaquina Bay in 1871. The area is named for the Yaquina tribe. The lighthouse, which exhibited a fifth-order lens, served the burgeoning lumber and oyster trade of central Oregon, but it was not well-positioned for ships to see it. Only four years into its career, it was decommissioned when a taller lighthouse replaced it on Yaquina Head a few miles to the north.

The lens was removed and placed in storage. Various tenants, including the U.S. Army, the U.S. Lifesaving Service, and the Coast Guard occupied the lighthouse over the next fifty years. After 1933 it was abandoned and became an eyesore in the community. Plans were made to raze it but the public objected. The lighthouse got a temporary reprieve when the Lincoln County Historical Society formed in 1948 and took charge of it.

However, the group was not able to raise enough money to restore the lighthouse, and it was again scheduled for the wrecking ball. Protests tabled the plan. By 1955 the historical society had raised the funds needed to open the lighthouse as a museum. In 1974 complete restoration began under the aegis of the Oregon Historical Society. In 1996 the lighthouse was relit with a 250mm optic with a range of 6 miles. It is a privately maintained official aid to navigation.

Today the site is a popular museum in the town of Newport. Displays depict the history of the area and the lighthouse. The Friends of Yaquina Lighthouses manages the site for the Oregon State Parks Association.

Maritime historian James Gibbs was photographed at Yaquina Bay Lighthouse in the early 1960s before restoration of the site. Returned to its former glory by the Oregon Historical Society, it is a popular Newport landmark today.

Yaquina Head Lighthouse   44.676N, 124.079W

FOR MORE INFORMATION
See information under
Yaquina Bay Lighthouse.

HOURS OF OPERATION
Interpretive Center hours and
lighthouse tour times vary.
Call 541.574.3100 for information.

DIRECTIONS
From Highway 101 three
miles north of Newport, turn
west at the sign for the lighthouse.

Oregon's tallest lighthouse is the stately 1873
sentinel on Yaquina Head.
Similar in design to California's Pigeon Point
Lighthouse, it replaced the
defunct Yaquina Bay Lighthouse, which lies a few
miles south inside the entrance to Yaquina Bay.

Rising 93 feet high, with
114 steps spiraling to the
lantern room, its first-order Fresnel lens cast
a fixed beam more than
20 miles at sea on clear
nights.

From 1873 to the 1920s,
two lightkeepers and their
families lived in a large
duplex and a third bachelor lightkeeper lived in a small outbuilding with no kitchen.

989   YAQUINA LIGHT HOUSE, YAQUINA HEAD

PHOTO BY WESLEY ANDREWS   OREGON COAST HIGHWAY

In 1922 a bungalow was added. (Both dwellings are shown in the postcard on the opposite page.) The station was much like a farm in its heyday, with a barn, a pasture for livestock, probably a chicken coop, and buildings associated with the lighthouse.

The lighthouse has always been a popular tourist stop. Its dramatic seascape and extensive tidepools draw visitors, as does the tall tower. Lightkeepers recorded as many as 600 visitors per day in the logbook in summer. In 1938 alone, a keeper reported that 12,000 people came to see the station. The following year the Coast Guard took over, razed the old Victorian house, and built new quarters.

By this time the station was electrified and the light

had a flashing characteristic. The beacon was automated in 1966, but Coast Guard personnel continued to live on site for a few years until all buildings but the tower and workroom were torn down. The site remained closed to the public until its transfer to the Bureau of Land Management in the 1990s. Today it is completely restored and includes a spacious parking area and visitor center. This is one of the most popular lighthouses in the nation, with about 400,000 visitors per year.

Lost Lights of the Columbia River

The dangerous entrance to the Columbia River—famous for its treacherous bar— and the first seventy miles of the river's interior have had many lights. Cape Disappointment Lighthouse was the first, inaugurated in 1856. It is still in operation. North Head Light, built in 1898, remains on duty as well, along with the 1889 Warrior Rock Lighthouse situated on the north end of an island in the river near the town of St. Helens, Oregon. The 1881 Tillamook Light, which marked the south approach to the river, was decommissioned in 1957. Other lighthouses, mostly on the Oregon shore where storms and the river's erosive powers are at their worst, came and went.

In 1875 a handsome Carpenter Gothic-style lighthouse was built at Point Adams on the Oregon side of the mouth of the Columbia

River. Its short career was fraught with problems. Mariners complained its fog signal was inaudible over the roar of surf. Sand constantly piled up around the lighthouse. In 1881, after Tillamook Light went into service and the signal of Point Adams Light was changed from flashing to a fixed light, a ship went aground nearby.

The fourth-order light continued in service, but without its useless foghorn. Month by month, erosion caused the river to creep closer to the lighthouse. Fences were tried to keep sand away from the structure, without success. In 1899 the lighthouse was abandoned and left to decay. It was a disheveled sight in 1912 when the Lighthouse Service burned it down. By then, it had been replaced with a light out in the river on Desdemona Sands.

Where the Megler Bridge now spans the Columbia River between Astoria, Oregon and Washington is a sandbank in the middle of the river. It has long been a navigational hazard. The first known vessel to wreck on the shoal was the bark *Desdemona*, which ran aground on January 1, 1857, despite the presence of buoys marking the shoal and its surrounding shallows. Thereafter, the sandbank was known as Desdemona Sands.

At one time the dry patch of Desdemona Sands was large enough to accommodate a farm and livestock. Ships entering the Columbia River and headed for Portland passed the shoal, as did ferries running between the Oregon and Washington shores.

In 1902 a lighthouse on stilts was built to mark the shallows. It consisted of a 1½ story octagonal wooden dwelling with a small lantern rising from its roof that exhibited a fourth-order lens 46 feet above the river. A foghorn protruded from the west wall, calling to ships entering the river. The sentinel sat on a platform supported by wooden piles.

Nature gradually wore down the pilings and slowly undermined the lighthouse. By World War II it was badly weathered.

The Coast Guard opted to tear down the lighthouse and replace it with a minor light on a wooden pyramidal structure. In 1955 this light was replaced by a pole light. The light was discontinued altogether in 1965. A footnote to the story concerns the lens, which was found in a private home in the 1990s and purchased for $10,000 by the Mukilteo Historical Society. It now sits on display in the base of the Mukilteo Lighthouse in Washington.

A near-twin to the Desdemona Sands sentinel was the Willamette River Lighthouse, built in 1895 at the junction of the Columbia and Willamette rivers in Portland. Though of the same design as Desdemona Sands Lighthouse, it exhibited a small beacon mounted on a post that rose from the gallery around the dwelling. There was also a fogbell. In 1935 the old lighthouse was deactivated and the light and bell were moved to a post near Kelley Point where they could be run on electricity. The abandoned lighthouse was sold to the Portland Mercantile Exchange and moved to shore. It burned down in the 1950s.

Today the river is marked by numerous modern pole lights. Every year the buoy tender *Henry Blake* makes a run up the river checking all the lights and buoys to be sure they are properly positioned and in good working order.

110

Range lights marked many of the twists and turns in the Columbia River. Ships steered a course that kept both beacons lined up to make the tricky turns in the river channel. One of the Flavel Range lights is shown as it appeared in 1949--a small automatic beacon atop a ring of pilings. It worked in tandem with a partner beacon farther downriver to help vessels negotiate a safe course past Portland. Today fiberglass pole beacons do the same job.

Cape Meares Lighthouse   45.486N, 123.97W

FOR MORE INFORMATION
Friends of Cape Meares
Lighthouse
P.O. Box 262
Oceanside, OR 97134
www.capemeareslighthouse.
org

HOURS OF OPERATION
Tours are given daily from
April through October, 11
A.M. to 4 P.M.

DIRECTIONS
From US 101 near Tillamook,
follow signs for Cape Meares
State Park and the lighthouse.
A broad trail leads down from
the parking area to the lighthouse and gift shop.

Cape Meares was first called Cape Lookout by Capt. John Meares on his travels through the area in 1788. Later, the cape was given his name when cartographers discov-ered maps with Cape Lookout in the wrong spot. Rather than make expensive corrections to maps and charts, the error was accepted and in 1857 the precipitous cliff overlooking Three Arches became known as Cape Meares.

The stocky, octagonal iron light tower at Cape Meares went into service in 1890 on an imposing cliff 215 feet above sea. The construction crew built a wooden crane from local fir trees and hauled materials up the cliff from the beach below. The 38-foot tower's iron sections were fitted together around a lining of brick. The first-order lens was disassembled and crated and brought by ship around Cape Horn, landed on the beach, and winched up to the light tower, where it was reassembled in the lantern. Two oil houses completed the functional part of the station.

Far up the hill behind the lighthouse were two keepers' dwellings and a barn. There was no road into the town of Tilla-mook until 1894. Keep-ers traveled by boat to fetch mail and supplies and relied on the tender

to bring many of the items they needed. A horseback trail was used through the woods when the tides or storms would not allow boat travel. The lighthouse children took the trail to school when it was passable.

A service room was added at the base of the tower in 1895. It was a long walk from the dwellings to the tower where keepers spent hours standing watch in the small room. Their duties were eased in 1934 when the lighthouse was electrified. In 1963 the first-order lens was shut down and an automatic modern optic was mounted on top of a square concrete building beside the tower. By then the homes for the keepers were gone, along with the oil houses and the service room.

The lighthouse was scheduled for demolition, but public protest resulted in its transfer to Tillamook County and Oregon State Parks. It sat vacant for a number of years and sections of the lens were stolen. The Friends of Cape Meares Lighthouse opened it for tours in 1980 and have been working slowly to restore the site. The service room was rebuilt and became a gift shop. In recent years, the station has undergone a facelift. Magically, lost parts of the lens have reappeared, left on the lighthouse doorstep or recovered from private homes. The lens was restored,

but tragedy struck again in January 2010 when vandals shot out lantern windows and damaged the lens. They were apprehended and arrested. The Friends of Cape Meares Lighthouse is currently raising funds to repair the lens.

Warrior Rock Lighthouse   45.848N, 122.788W

DIRECTIONS

Sauvie Island can be accessed from the Oregon shore via a small bridge off Highway 30 north of Linnton. Once on the island take NW Sauvie Island Road to a right turn at Reeder Road. Follow Reeder Road to its terminus and then hike about 3 miles to the lighthouse.

On October 28, 1792, Lieutenant William Broughton led a small party of explorers from Captain George Vancouver's ship *Discovery* to Sauvie Island in the Columbia River. Soon after arriving at the north end of the island, Broughton found himself surrounded by twenty-three canoes of fierce-looking Chinooks. He signaled his desire for peace and quickly left, calling the place "Warrior Rock."

In 1889 a small lighthouse was built on Warrior Rock. The first floor was the dwelling, but the keeper did not live there. Instead, he lived ashore and rowed to the light daily to tend it. On top of the small tower, accessible by a ladder, were a work room and the lantern. A lens-lantern was mounted on the peak, and a fogbell cast in Philadelphia in 1855 hung off to the side of the structure, facing the river. The bell had served at  Cape Disappointment Lighthouse on the Washington side of the entrance to the Columbia River and also at West Point Light in Seattle. Though the bell had an automatic striker, the mechanism broke down frequently and the keeper had to ring the bell by hand.

When the Columbia River ran high with spring snowmelt, the base of the lighthouse was usually awash, making it difficult for the keeper to climb aboard. Eventually, the wooden tower deteriorated and a new lighthouse was built. A 28-foot-tall concrete sentinel was erected on the old foundation. The fogbell was mounted on it, along with a modern beacon. It ran automatically and served until 1969 when a barge traveling down the river rammed it.

The Coast Guard removed the historic old bell, repaired the tower, and placed the sentinel back in service. The bell was cracked as it was being taken ashore. It now sits on the grounds of the courthouse in St. Helens, Oregon. A half-size replica of the original lighthouse sits on the river side of the courthouse.

Coast Guard electricians conducted maintenance on War-rior Rock Lighthouse in 1960. Orange triangular day boards were mounted on either side of the lighthouse, and it sported a small beacon on a pole.

Tillamook Rock Lighthouse   45.937N, 124.019W

DIRECTIONS
The lighthouse is visible from Ecola State Park off Highway 101 just north of Cannon Beach.

Nicknamed "Terrible Tilly" by lightkeepers of the past who dreaded duty on the isolated 1881 sentinel, Tillamook Rock is the only offshore lighthouse in Oregon. It takes its name from the native Tillamook tribe of the area.

Construction of the lighthouse, which took almost two years, tested the mettle of the architects and workmen. The tower was lighted for the first time on January 1, 1881 with a first-order lens that shone from 133 feet above sea. There was also a foghorn. The sentinel was tasked with guiding ships in and out of the Columbia River entrance.

Five keepers were assigned to the lonely lighthouse. Their families lived ashore, since the site was too dangerous for women and children. The duty was demanding and sometimes hazardous. During severe storms, spray washed over the lighthouse and powerful waves sent rocks flying into it. A storm in October 1934 battered the lighthouse and threw a large rock into the lantern, breaking the lens. An auxiliary light was set up and the ruined lens was scrapped.

In 1957 the light was discontinued and its duties were transferred to a large whistle buoy with a red beacon. The tower was sold and passed through the hands of several private own-

HALE 261.   Tillamook Light - Oregon Coast

ers until the 1980s when it was purchased by a real estate company and opened as the Eternity at Sea columbarium. The company lost its license in 1999 because of complaints about methods of storage and protection of the urns. At this writing the company is still seeking renewal of the license.

The lighthouse is inaccessible at the present time and is not open to the public.

A supply tender approached Tillamook Light (previous page) in rough seas about 1940. The tender always anchored off the rock and sent a small boat to the landing, where it was winched up by derrick. Landings were difficult in winter months. The public's fascination with the lighthouse was fueled by images such as this one and a plethora of postcards (above) showing waves breaking against the rockbound sentinel.

Excerpts from Lighthouse Logbooks

Lightkeepers were required to keep records of activities at their stations, including weather reports, tasks completed, tallies of fuel used and hours the fog signals ran, visitors to the station, arrival and departure of crew members, and equipment installation, malfunction, and repair. While the ability to read and write was required, not all keepers were good at spelling and grammar, as the following excerpts show. Their logbooks do reveal the everyday routine of lighthouses, punctuated by the occasional storm or other unusual occurrence. Occasionally an unexpected entry was made—a poem, a sketch of a bird, tidbits of wisdom.

3278 - Cape Foulweather Lighthouse, Oregon

Yaquina Head Lighthouse, Oregon

December 31, 1878: ...the 31st was clear and fine again so ends the year 1878 at Cape Foulweather and the record shows it is not always foul weather...

March 2, 1879: From 6 to 12 midnight heavy gale S. to S.W. light rain remainder of 24 hours fresh to moderate breeze S.W. to West during the first 6 hours the wind hurld [sic] small pebbles against the windows with such force that 18 or 20 panes of glass were broken in the Storm windows blew open some 40 feet of picket fence and a portion of shingles from the Oil house sea rough.

June 8, 1887: Keepers whitewashing the garden fence and weeding the garden also today.

October 24, 1891: 1st Asst. went Geese hunting.

Smith Island Lighthouse, Washington

March 22, 1882: At 8:30 a.m. the house was discovered to be on fire, at the west end, by the chimney. It was soon put out, not doing very serious damage. It was found, upon examination, to have taken fire on the inside, next to the chimney, and must have been smoldering some time before it broke out.
DeWitt Dennison, Keeper

October 27, 1891: DeWitt Dennison, keeper of Smith Island Light Station died and was taken to Whidbey Island and buried.
Frank Dennison, Acting Keeper

Willapa Bay Lighthouse, Washington

August 28, 1893: Sent for the Doctor this morning. Baby being very sick. Doctor staid all night. Dr. pronounced the children's sickness Scarlet Fever.

September 4, 1893: I am going to leave the station today to go up to Willapa with the body of my stepdaughter to bury it in the Fernhill Cemetery. Will be gone for two days. Went out to the graveyard this morning and exhumed the body.

M.A. Stream, Keeper

Admiralty Head Lighthouse, Washington

August 28, 1874: Within the last two or three days, several barks have passed going up and down the Sound. This morning to came in quite close bound up but drifting—toward night a fresh breeze sprang up from the west and with the turning of the tide the two barks sailed up to the Sound—one was the Aureola—name discernible with a glass.

Flora Pearson, Assistant Keeper

St. George Reef Light Station

May 13, 1974: After four score and three years, St. George Reef Light is dark. No longer will your bright beams of light be seen, nor your bellowing fog signal be heard by the mariner. Gone are your keepers. Only by your faithful service has many a disaster been prevented on the treacherous St. George Reef. You stand today as you have down through the years, a tribute to humanity and worthy of our highest respect. Cut from the soul of our country, you have valiantly earned your place in America's history. In your passing, the era of the lonely sea sentinel has truly ended. May Mother Nature show you mercy. You have been abandoned, but never will you be forgotten. Farewell, St. George Reef Light.

J. LeCoslin, Officer-in-Charge

Tillamook Rock Lighthouse, Oregon

May 20, 1882: Heavy northerly wind clear and warm. Launched the boat and went to one of the moorings and tried to catch a fish, "not even a bite," no meat, no coffee, no sugar, no pickles, and no fish in fact we have nothing but dissatisfaction at the way we are treated. Steamer Shubrick came to the rock at 7 PM too rough to land went to Anchor at Arch Rock.

December 9, 1894: Heavy seas started at 11 AM came over tower 10 plates glass were broken.

December 12, 1894: First warm meal since 9th.

December 13, 1894: Columbine arrived but could not land delivered news in a bottle.

July 19, 1899: Lassold a big bull sea lion early this morning, weight 2,000 lbs.

124

Lighthouse keeping often was a lonely, thankless occupation. Keepers worked long hours, especially when the fog signal was operating, and received little time off. Point Reyes Light Station, despite its large crew, was often a forlorn and friendless place. Few visitors came, and the hardship of life at the foggy, wind-swept site sometimes caused silence among its occupants. Perhaps this is what spurred lightkeeper E.G. Chamberlain in 1885 to quote English poet William Cowper:

> *Solitude, where are the charms that sages have seen in thy face?*
>
> *Better to dwell in the midst of alarms than reign in this horrible place.*
>
> *So city, friendship, and love,*
>
> *Divinely bestowed upon man,*
>
> *O' had I the wings of a dove,*
>
> *How I would taste you again...*

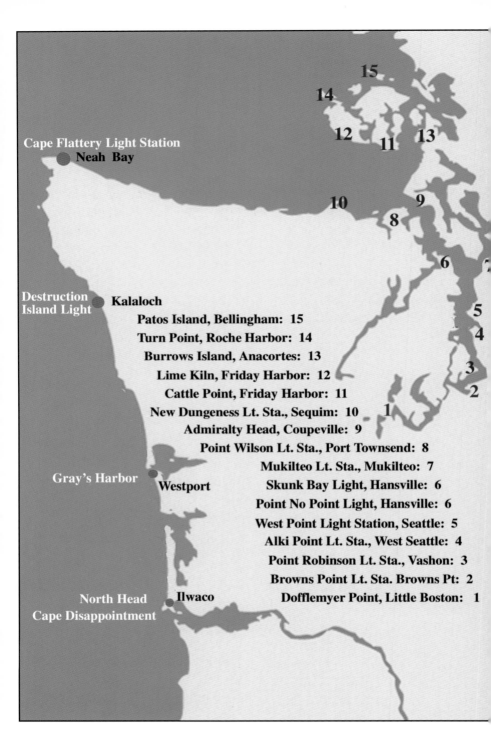

Cape Flattery Light Station
Neah Bay

Destruction Island Light   Kalaloch

Patos Island, Bellingham: 15
Turn Point, Roche Harbor: 14
Burrows Island, Anacortes: 13
Lime Kiln, Friday Harbor: 12
Cattle Point, Friday Harbor: 11
New Dungeness Lt. Sta., Sequim: 10
Admiralty Head, Coupeville: 9
Point Wilson Lt. Sta., Port Townsend: 8

Gray's Harbor   Westport

Mukilteo Lt. Sta., Mukilteo: 7
Skunk Bay Light, Hansville: 6
Point No Point Light, Hansville: 6
West Point Light Station, Seattle: 5
Alki Point Lt. Sta., West Seattle: 4
Point Robinson Lt. Sta., Vashon: 3
Browns Point Lt. Sta. Browns Pt: 2
North Head   Ilwaco   Dofflemyer Point, Little Boston: 1
Cape Disappointment

Lighthouses of Washington

No lighthouse greeted Captain George Vancouver as his ships explored the foggy coast of present-day Washington in 1792, nor did a beacon guide Lewis and Clark in 1804 on their landmark journey to the mouth of the Columbia River. A half-century would pass before Washington became a territory of the United States and pioneers began arriving in droves to fish, cut timber, and homestead. With only crude trails providing access to settlements, and the Olympic and Cascade Mountains a forbidding obstacle to travelers, Washington's waterways became its highways. Plans were made to tame its wild shores with lighthouses.

The first official navigational light went into service at Cape Disappointment in 1856 to mark the Columbia River Bar, one of the world's most daunting shipping obstacles. Lights also went into service at Willapa Bay, a busy oyster and lumber port, and at Cape Flattery, Dungeness Spit, and Smith Island in the Strait of Juan de Fuca. By the 1880s the inside waters of Puget Sound had been marked from Point No Point south to Olympia. After Washington became a state in 1889, the dangerous islands of the San Juan archipelago also received lights.

With the exception of the brick tower at Cape Disappointment, Washington's early sentinels were fashioned after the Cape Cod-style lighthouses of California. The towers rose from simple dwellings. Fogbells or stream signals sounded warnings through the frequent mists. Toward the end of the nineteenth century and up until about 1920, Astoria architect Carl Leick was the dean of lighthouse construction throughout the Pacific Northwest. His designs usually incorporated a tower and fog signal in a brick or concrete structure coated in parge, a stucco-like mixture that provided protection in the wet climate.

Twenty-six lighthouses and three lightships were established in Washington between 1856 and 1914. Many were rebuilt after the elements caused them to deteriorate or the shorelines changed. Several, including the lights at Willapa Bay, Ediz Hook, and Slip Point, washed away and were replaced by steel skeleton towers. Twenty traditional lighthouses still stand in the Evergreen State, most still operational.

Washington's lightkeepers came largely from local communities and brought their families to the stations. The keeper with the longest tenure was John Cowan, who served at Cape Flattery Lighthouse from 1900 to 1932. He had previously served at two Oregon lighthouses. Several women also held lightkeeping jobs, including Mabel Bretherton of North Head Lighthouse and the Smith sisters of Ediz Hook Light, as well as famed "Mercer Girl" Flora Pearson who came to the Seattle area with the Mercer Expedition in 1866 to help even out the ratio of men to women in the Northwest and ended up serving as an assistant keeper at Red Bluff Lighthouse.

The Coast Guard, which took control of navigational aids in 1939, began modernizing and automating the lighthouses and fog signals in Washington. The last station to have a lightkeeper was West Point Light in Seattle; it was automated in 1985.

Following automation, many of the state's lighthouses were leased or transferred to federal, state, municipal, and nonprofit groups. Thirteen lighthouses and one lightship are open to the public as museums, overnight rentals, or attractions in parks. The Washington Lightkeepers Association serves as a clearinghouse for information on the state's lighthouses and lightships and plans annual events to celebrate their history and lore. Write to the group at P.O. Box 984, Seabeck, WA 98380 or visit their website at www.walightkeepers.com.

*By 1870 when this photograph was taken, Cape Disappoint-
ment exhibited a first-order light and was a beehive of activity.
The lighthouse—the first in Washington—shared its site with Fort
Canby and a fledgling lifesaving station. Cannons were lined up
east of the tower, overlooking the Columbia River and ready to
fire if needed. In the hollow below the cape, an all-volunteer crew
of surfmen launched a lifeboat when needed to aid ships in distress. A fogbell hung in a wooden frame next to the work shed, but
practice drills with the cannons had nearly destroyed the building
housing the bell's striking mechanism. Within a few years the bell
was removed and taken to West Point Light in Seattle.*

Cape Disappointment Lighthouse 46.27N, 124.05W

FOR MORE INFORMATION
Washington Parks & Recreational Commission, Long Beach Area
P.O. Box 488
Ilwaco, WA 98624
www.parks.wa.gov/lcinterpctr.asp

DIRECTIONS
From US 101 at Ilwaco, follow signs south to Fort Canby State Park. View the lighthouse from the Lewis & Clark Interpretive Center or walk the park trail to the tower.

Captain John Meares sought shelter on the north side of the mouth of the Columbia River in July 1788 but was disappointed he could not escape rough water. He named the headland Cape Disappointment. Later, the headland was marked by a flagpole, and sailing directions noted that it had several distinguishable trees. Finally, in 1856, a lighthouse was built on the cape. It was one of the earliest lighthouses on the West Coast and is the oldest lighthouse in Washington.

The 53-foot brick tower stood on a high bluff overlooking the treacherous Columbia River bar where many shipwrecks occurred. It exhibited a first-order Fresnel lens from an elevation of 225 feet. A fogbell was mounted in a frame building in front of the tower. About a quarter-mile back from the cliff in a protected hollow away from the cape's insistent wind was a keeper's dwelling.

Fort Canby was built on the cape during the Civil War, and cannons were set up around the lighthouse. By 1871, percussion from cannon fire had destroyed the fogbell building, and the fog signal was discontinued.

A lifesaving effort to aid shipwrecks was begun in the 1870s by lightkeeper Joel Munson. It was later incorporated into the U.S. Lifesaving Service and then the Coast Guard, which today trains its lifesavers and rescue swimmers at Coast Guard Station Cape Disappointment near the footprint of the old keeper's dwelling.

In 1898 the first-order lens was transferred to nearby North Head Lighthouse and a fourth-order lens was installed at Cape Disappointment Light. It was eventually automated, but the Coast Guard continued using the lighthouse as a lookout over the dangerous Columbia River bar.

The lighthouse is closed to visitors but the grounds are open during daylight hours as part of Cape Disappointment State Park. Park rangers open the lighthouse for tours on special occasions. Exhibits, including the first-order lens, are on display at the park's Lewis & Clark Interpretive Center.

FOR MORE INFORMATION
Cape Disappointment State Park
360.642.3029
www.northheadlighthouse.com

DIRECTIONS
From Ilwaco, follow signs to
Fort Canby State Park. Turn
right at the sign for the lighthouse, park in the designated
area, and hike about a quarter-
mile to the lighthouse.

North Head, as its name implies, marks the elevated northern headland at the entrance to the Columbia River. The Spanish-style 65-foot brick lighthouse was built in 1898 in response to increased shipping into Seattle and ports in Alaska. It also worked in tandem with Cape Disappointment Light to help vessels enter the treacherous Columbia River bar.

Two spacious keepers' dwellings stood on the hill behind the tower, away from the wind. There was also a mule barn, a chicken coop, and several work buildings. A long path led from the homes to the lighthouse and work buildings on the point. On stormy days the keepers could barely walk on the point. It was not unusual to have steady winds of 40 to 50 miles per hour, and storm winds could top 100 miles per hour. During the Great Olympic Blowdown in 1921, named for the vast stands of trees lost to the wind, the lighthouse clocked a gust of 126 miles per hour.

The station's first-order lens, which had been relocated from Cape Disappointment Lighthouse in 1898, served until 1935 when electricity was installed. The fourth-order lens that replaced it was exhibited until the 1950s when two rotating aerobeacons took over. The station was automated in 1961 and, later, an auxiliary light was placed on the lantern gallery as a backup beacon.

The lighthouse was transferred to Washington State Parks in 2012. Keepers of North Head Lighthouse manages a small gift shop and conducts tours of the tower. The grounds are open as part of Cape Disappointment State Park, and the dwellings are popular vacation rentals managed by the park.

Sunsets at North Head Light Station often are spectacular. Skywatchers know it's a great place to see the Green Flash, a sky phenomenon that occurs on clear days at sunset when the last bit of the sun's disk disappears over the horizon in a brilliant emerald flash of light.

Grays Harbor Lighthouse   46.888N, 124.116W

FOR MORE INFORMATION
Westport Maritime Museum
P.O. Box 1074
Westport, WA 98595
360.268.0078
www.westportwa.com/mu-
seum

DIRECTIONS
From SR105 in Westport,
turn left on Ocean Avenue
and drive about a half mile to
the viewing platform on the
right. Tours of the lighthouse
are available from Westport
Maritime Museum on West-
haven Drive in Westport.

The tallest lighthouse in Washington marks historic Grays Harbor, named for Captain Robert Gray, who explored the area in 1792. The harbor, which is formed by the outflow of the Chehalis River, has a dangerous bar and is fraught with persistent fogs, wind, and heavy seas during storms. The Lighthouse Board vacillated about whether to build a seacoast light on the beach or a harbor light at the mouth of the estuary. The seacoast won, so the imposing lighthouse was built in 1898 to guide vessels to the big lumber operations at Aberdeen and Hoquiam.

The 107-foot brick tower wore a beige daymark and later was painted white and green. Its unusual Fresnel lens combined a set of third-order panels and a half clamshell. An oil house and a storage shed flanked the base of the tower. The site also included two dwellings and a windmill to provide water for the steam fog signal.

The dwellings and fog signal building were removed by the late 1960s when the lighthouse was automated. By this time changes to the shoreline had left the lighthouse some distance from the shore, and trees had grown up around the station. Still, the tower was tall enough to be seen by vessels at sea.

In 1992 the magnificent Henry-LaPaute lens, made in France, was turned off and a modern beacon was installed on the tower's lantern railing to replace it. Six years later the Westport-South Beach Historical Society leased the lighthouse for public tours. It was formally conveyed to the society through the National Historic Lighthouse Preservation Act in 2004.

Destruction Island Lighthouse   47.67N, 124.486W

FOR MORE INFORMATION
See Grays Harbor Lighthouse for information about Westport Maritime Museum and the first-order lens display. For information on the marine sanctuary go to www.olym-piccoast.noaa.gov

DIRECTIONS
U.S. Fish & Wildlife regulations forbid visits to the lighthouse because of endangered species living on Destruction Island. It can be viewed from several pullouts along Highway 101 near Ruby Beach and Kalaloch.

Known to local residents as DI, the 94-foot lighthouse was built in 1891 on the grassy plateau of a 30-acre island three miles from shore. The island earned its terrible name in the late 1700s when explorers anchored there and sent crewman ashore for food and fresh water. The men were killed by the fierce native Quinaults. The Spanish dubbed the island the "Isla de Dolores," or Island of Sorrows. The British later called it Destruction Island.

Ships traveling the Washington coast had to stay well offshore to avoid Destruction Island, as it was difficult to see in fogs and stormy weather. Shipping interests lobbied for a lighthouse for decades before funds became available for the costly project. The exterior of the new 94-foot-tall lighthouse was fortified with a sheath of iron to protect it from the wind and rain that assails the island. It exhibited a 24-panel first-order flashing Fresnel lens that rotated on chariot wheels. There was also a steam fog signal, a cistern for water storage, two oil houses, two dwellings, and a barn.

The isolated island challenged its four keepers and their families. Winter storms slammed the station with powerful winds, the worst gusts clocked at over 100 miles per hour. The island's dense forest was quickly leveled for fuel and the deer population was decimated to keep the larder filled. Livestock was lost over the cliffs, and children had to be carefully watched. Sometimes life was comedic, as when a lone bull on the island mistook a new foghorn for a rival bull and went on a mad spree, attacking buildings, oil tanks, and people.

Difficulty landing supplies made the station one of the first in Washington to be de-staffed. It was automated in 1968, and most of the station buildings were razed. In 1995, after more than a century of service to mariners, the opulent Fresnel lens was dismantled and replaced by a modern solar optic. The lens was moved to Westport Maritime Museum for display.

In 2008 a budget-strapped Coast Guard extinguished the light altogether and sealed it up as much as possible against vandalism. Today it sits dark and quiet, a part of the Olympic Coast National Marine Sanctuary. The island is off limits to the public.

Lightkeeper Al Beyer posed for a photograph in front of his luminous charge about 1940. He wore work dungarees and a lightkeeper's hat. Beyer's little girl had a pet fawn named Bambi that was brought to the island from the mainland.

Cape Flattery Light Station   48.39N, 124.736W

DIRECTIONS
The island is off limits to the public. A viewpoint can be accessed via the 0.75 mile long, wood plank Cape Flattery Trail from a parking area six miles west of Neah Bay off state road 112.

Established in 1857 on Tatoosh Island at the northwest tip of Washington, the 65-foot brick lighthouse marks the entrance to the Strait of Juan de Fuca. The island is named for Chief Tatoosh of the Makah tribe. The Makah used the island as a fish processing center and burial ground. In 1792 Captain George Vancouver dubbed the place Cape Flattery, noting that it "flattered" him to think he might have found the fabled Northwest Passage here.

The lighthouse originally exhibited a first-order lens. A fog-bell house and a spacious two-story dwelling also were built. Four keepers shared the quarters in the base of the lighthouse. It was miserable, lonely duty. The house was cold and leaky. Getting on and off the island involved a derrick and crate that was raised and lowered from the island plateau. Rough weather often prevented the keepers from getting ashore and the lighthouse tender from making regular stops at the island. Mail and supplies had to be delivered by an intrepid canoe paddler from the Makah settlement at Neah Bay.

A steam fog signal replaced the bell in 1871. A short time later a new duplex dwelling was built. A weather station was added to the site in 1883, and in the 1920s the Navy installed a Radio Compass Station. A few years later the first-order lens was replaced by a fourth-order optic. More buildings were erected, and by the 1930s a small community of about thirty people lived on the island.

There was even a schoolhouse and a live-in teacher. But everyone was gone by 1977 when the station was automated with a modern, self-sufficient optic.

The lighthouse underwent extensive repairs in the 1990s. It was taken out of service in 2009 and the beacon was moved to a metal tower on the west side of the lighthouse. The site was returned to the Makah tribe. It sits within a marine sanctuary.

The fourth-order lens is on display at the Clallam County Museum in Port Angeles. Only a section of the first-order lens remains; it can be seen in the collection of the Museum of Labor and Industry in Seattle.

Dofflemyer Point Lighthouse   47.14N, 122.907W

DIRECTIONS
The light is not open to the public. It can be seen from the boat ramp and marina in the small community of Boston Harbor.

In 1887 a 12-foot-high wharf post light was set up on the northeast side of Budd Inlet, an important turning point for ships headed in and out of the port of Olympia. The site was Dofflemyer Point, a shoal-ridden area named for a pioneer who settled on the point in the early 1860s. A local resident was hired to maintain the beacon, along with two other minor lights in the area. As Olympia grew, complaints about the maze of waterways leading to it mounted. The port was not a high priority for the Lighthouse Service funding sources in faraway Washington, D.C., but finally, in 1934, the post light was upgraded and placed on a 34-foot octagonal concrete tower with a tiny iron lantern on top. Inside the lantern was a small drum lens illuminated with an electric bulb. An electric air horn was added as a fog signal.

Unlike most lighthouses, Dofflemyer Point was serviced by a contract keeper who lived nearby. For many years the lighthouse and fog signal was tended by a local woman named Madeleine Campbell, whose beach home was beside the lighthouse. The light was automated in the 1960s with a plastic optic. The small lantern was removed. The horn was manually operated by Campbell for another twenty years before it, too, was made self-sufficient. In 1987 a radiobeacon was added to the lighthouse to further assist mariners.

In 2006 the Coast Guard removed the historic fog signal, much to the dismay of the Little Boston neighborhood. It was no longer needed, and there was no response to the "Notice to Mariners" the Coast Guard published. A small grassroots group in the town hopes to have the foghorn reinstated. The light remains active and is visible for 9 miles. It sits on a private beach but can be seen from a nearby marina.

In 2004, Dofflemyer Lighthouse still had its fog signal. The fog detector can be seen on the top of the lighthouse, a box-like structure on a pole at left. The foghorn is the low, round structure in the center, and the beacon rises above the fog signal equipment.

The Lighthouse Service Bulletin

Reading has always been associated with lighthouse keeping. Keepers loved books and magazines; these were donated to lighthouses by various charities. Portable libraries were issued to lighthouses and regularly exchanged. Beginning in 1912, the newly-formed U.S. Bureau of Lighthouses, under the superintendence of George R. Putnam, began publishing a monthly newsletter on a variety of topics of interest to its employees. Putnam's goal was to keep the vast number of employees in the bureau informed, educated, entertained, and united. The bulletin was sent to all lighthouse and lightship personnel, crews of tenders, workers in the many depots, and administrative staff. *The Lighthouse Service Bulletin* was issued monthly until 1939 when the Coast Guard assumed control of lighthouses. A few excerpts from the publication follow:

Lighthouse Service Bulletin

ISSUED   *MONTHLY*

February 1924

On December 7, 1923, huge seas from a west-northwesterly direction broke on the platform at St. George Reef Light Station, Calif., 70 feet above water, with such violence as to tear the donkey engine house from its foundations and move it over against the coping of the dock. All steam pipes, water pipes, and hoisting derrick control levers were either broken or badly damaged by the seas. No damage of this character has been reported from the station before, and it appears probable that this constitutes a record for heavy seas at the station. The keeper was ashore at the time and was unable to return to the station for a period of nearly two weeks, but during that time he was in daily communication with the other keepers at the station by means of the recently installed radiotelephone at the light and at Crescent City.

Lighthouse Service Bulletin

ISSUED   *MONTHLY*

December 1931

New Dungeness Light Station is located on a low, narrow sand spit extending about 4 miles into the Strait of Juan de Fuca, Wash., and due to climatic changes has become one of the driest spots in the Puget Sound country. Several years ago a large watershed was constructed at the light station, and rain water, collected from the rain shed and dwellings and stored, provided the station with fresh water. However, in recent years, with the addition of modern plumbing and sanitary systems, this supply of water has been found entirely inadequate for the station needs.

In 1930 the possibility of drilling an artesian well at the station was investigated, and favorable reports were received...Operations were started in September 1930, ... drilling... to a total depth of 665 feet, a clay bed was penetrated and a sand and gravel water-bearing strata encountered....an artesian flow of 80 gallons per minute developed. The flow of water is entirely adequate for all present and future needs of the light station and when piped to the New Dungeness Light Station wharf will provide fresh water for lightships and tenders when required.

Lighthouse Service Bulletin

ISSUED   *MONTHLY*

December 1934

On September 1 the Fort Point Light Station, probably the second light to be established in California, was discontinued....Discontinuance of Fort Point is brought about by the erection of the new Golden Gate Bridge, the north pylon of which has been constructed outside the fog signal and light, cutting them off from vessels passing through the Golden Gate. The headland at Fort Point and the offlying shoal are now marked by a light and fog signal maintained jointly by the State Highway Commission and the contractor, and when the bridge is completed these aids will be permanently located on the main bridge pier....
In excavating for this pier the adobe walls of a portion of the old Spanish fort were uncovered. These structures were probably among the first to be erected on San Francisco Bay.

Browns Point Light Station   47.30N, 122.44W

FOR MORE INFORMATION
Points NE Historical Society
1000 Towne Center NE, PMB 135
Browns Point, WA 98422
bplighthouse@hotmail.com
www.pnehs.dreamhosters.com/
lighthouse
253.927.2536

DIRECTIONS
From Interstate 5, take exit 137
and go north to the exit for state
road 509 (Marine View Drive).
Drive about five miles to a small
shopping village and a sign for
Browns Point. Turn left and follow this road to the lighthouse.

A lens-lantern hoisted on top of a wooden post served as the first beacon for the Port of Tacoma. It was light-ed in 1887 on Point Brown at the eastern entrance to Com-mencement Bay. In 1903 the lens-lantern was moved to a two-story wooden tower that also housed a fogbell, one that had served at several other lighthouses in Wash-ington. A keeper's house was built behind the tower. There also was an oil house and boathouse.

The first and longest-serving keeper was Oscar Brown. A music teacher, he brought a piano to the station and gave private lessons in his free time. He also brought his horse and cow. The piano had been ardu-ously hauled ashore by the crew of the lighthouse tender. The horse and cow were pushed over the side of the ship and swam to their new home. Brown was keep-er of the lighthouse for 36 years.

The station was electrified in 1922, the same year it became known as Browns Point. Elev-en years later, the deteriorating wooden lighthouse was burned down and replaced by a reinforced concrete Art Deco Moderne style tower with a modern optic. An electric foghorn was installed, and the old fogbell was given to a local college. The new light-house required little care and eventually was automated in 1963.

The following year the lighthouse grounds became a public park. The Points Northeast Historical Society acquired and restored the keeper's cottage in 1998 and opened it as a vacation rental. A museum is housed in the basement. The boathouse also contains displays. The lighthouse is closed but the grounds are open daily during daylight hours as part of Tacoma's Metropolitan Parks District. The cottage is open for tours on select dates in December and August.

Point Robinson Light Station   47.388N, 122.37W

FOR MORE INFORMATION
Keepers of Point Robinson
P.O. Box 13234
Burton, WA 98013
For rental information, call
206.463.9602
lodging@vashonparkdistrict.org

HOURS OF OPERATION
Tours of the lighthouse are offered on Sundays from 12:00 P.M. to 4:00 P.M, Memorial Day through Labor Day. An open house is held in early December, with both rental dwellings open and tours of the lighthouse.

DIRECTIONS
From Point Defiance in Tacoma, take the ferry to Vashon Island and turn left off the ferry ramp onto Vashon Highway. Follow the highway to a right turn on Quartermaster Road. Turn right onto Dockton Road. At the Y, bear left onto Point Robinson Road and continue to the lighthouse.

Established in 1885 as a fog signal station, Point Robinson, with its steam whistle, helped ships navigate the East Passage between Seattle and Tacoma. Mariners had nicknamed the murky waterway "The Fog Net." A single dwelling for the fog signal keeper was built south of the fog signal building. A barn stood even farther south and a chicken coop sat near it.

In 1891, a 25-foot framework tower surmounted by a lens-lantern was added to the station, but it proved too short to be seen over the trees south of the point. It was relocated to a taller wooden scaffold tower three years later. The additional work created by the light required a second keeper, whose dwelling was built in 1907.

In 1915 the light and fog signal were combined into a single 38-foot-tall structure. The new lighthouse held a fifth-order lens and was a near-twin of its sister sentry at Alki Point. Three steam foghorns facing north, east, and south operated until electrification and the installation of electric horns. A walkway led from the boat landing to the lighthouse in order to transport coal and kerosene to a new oil house next to the tower. In 1917 the original dwelling was rebuilt.

The station was automated in the 1980s and later leased to Vashon Park District. It served as a private residence for a time before being converted to a vacation rental. Both dwellings are rented throughout the year. The north dwelling is retro-furnished to reflect the 1920s period when the station was in its heyday. The old garage has been converted to a gift shop.

In 2008 the fog signal was discontinued. A year later the light was removed from the antique fifth-order lens and relocated to a modern beacon on the lantern railing. The Keepers of Point Robinson, who maintain the site in conjunction with Vashon Park District, use a low-intensity light in the lens on special occasions. In 2011 vandals stole the defunct fog signal.

Alki Point Light Station   47.576N, 122.42W

HOURS OF OPERATION
Open Saturdays and Sundays, June through August, 1 P.M. to 4 P.M., except Fourth of July weekend. Call 206.841.3519 for more information.

DIRECTIONS
From Interstate 5, take exit 163 onto the West Seattle Freeway. At SW Admiral Way turn right, and then take another right onto 63rd Avenue. Turn right again on Alki Avenue and drive to the lighthouse parking area. A short walk south leads to the beach and views of the station.

In 1868, seventeen years after the first pioneers landed on Alki Beach on the south side of Elliot Bay, a crude lantern on a pole served as a light for ships headed into the growing port of Seattle. It was a beneficent service provided by two local landowners concerned about the safety of vessels entering and leaving the bay. The point was called Alki by its earliest settlers, after a Chinook word meaning "by and by, sooner or later." The nickname was a reference to the pioneers' disappointment with their new rainy home and a feeling they would someday learn to like it.

THE ALKI POINT LIGHTHOUSE, SEATTLE, U.S.A.

In 1887 the light at Alki Point was improved with the construction of a wooden scaffold that exhibited a lens-lantern. The lantern's kerosene reservoir held eight days of fuel and was tended by a lamplighter—Hans Hanson, one of the landowners who had helped establish the first lamp on the point. The lens-lantern operated until 1913 when a small parcel of land on the point was purchased from Hanson and an integrated light tower and fog signal building was constructed.

The 37-foot concrete tower had a fourth-order Fresnel lens made in Paris by the lens firm of Sautter & Lemmonier. Three fog trumpets projected from the lighthouse and blared over the water to the north, west, and south of the point, giving coverage to the foggy entrance to the East Passage leading to the port at Tacoma. Behind the lighthouse were an oil house and two comfortable dwellings for the keepers.

The lighthouse served uneventfully with two resident lightkeepers for forty-seven years and a Coast Guard keeper for another two decades. In the 1960s the lens was removed and a modern optic was installed. The entire station was automated in 1984.

Today the residences are home to Coast Guard families. Though the homes are off limits to visitors, the tower is open on summer Sunday afternoons. The lighthouse is difficult to see from the street but is visible from the beach. The original Fresnel lens is on display at Admiralty Head Lighthouse. The 1868 lens-lantern is on exhibit at the Coast Guard Museum Northwest.

West Point Light Station   47.66N, 122.435W

DIRECTIONS

The site is not open to the public at present but can be viewed from the beach in Discovery Park. Visitors can walk or bike to the beach from the parking area. In summer a shuttle bus runs from the parking area to the beach.

The lighthouse was placed in operation in 1881 on a jutting point at the base of Magnolia Hill to guide shipping into Elliott Bay. It sits on the west side of the entrance to the port of Seattle in Discovery Park. It is a twin of Point No Point Lighthouse.

The 27-foot tower exhibited a flashing fourth-order Fresnel lens. Ruby panels on alternating faces of the lens created a white and red flash. Behind the lighthouse a fogbell that had formerly served at Cape Disappointment Lighthouse hung in a wooden scaffold. In 1887, when the bell was replaced by a coal-fired steam fog trumpet, a fog signal building was added to the tower. The station also had two dwellings and an oil house.

Fort Lawton was built on the bluff behind the lighthouse by 1900, and in 1915 the Lake Washington Ship Canal opened at nearby Shilshole, increasing the light's importance.

In 1981 West Point Light's last keeper, Marvin Gerbers, celebrated the station's 100th birthday by climbing onto the roof of the lighthouse and pouring champagne on it. Gerbers left a final entry in the logbook in 1985 when the light was automated—the last one in Washington to be unmanned. It was given a new electric foghorn at this time.

In 2004 the site was transferred to Seattle City Parks through the National Historic Lighthouse Preservation Act. The city is currently restoring the station and plans to eventually open it for public use. The light in the lens has been discontinued and moved to a modern beacon on the lantern railing. The fog signal also has been discontinued.

The composite lighthouse at West Point includes (above) a fog signal building with horns mounted on the roof, a 27-foot tower, a workroom, and an oilhouse. The horns and beautiful fourth-order Fresnel lens have been decommissioned since this photo was taken, and the beacon now shines from a small plastic optic mounted on the lantern railing.

Point No Point Lighthouse   47.91N, 122.526W

FOR MORE INFORMATION
U.S. Lighthouse Society
9005 Point No Point Rd. NE
Hansville, WA 98340
415.362.7255
www.uslhs.org
info@uslhs.org

HOURS OF OPERATION
The society headquarters
and research library are
open weekdays by appoint-
ment. The vacation rental
is open year-round. Call
415.362.7255. Lighthouse
tours are Sundays from 12:00
P.M. to 4:00 P.M., Memorial
Day through Labor Day.

DIRECTIONS
From Tacoma, take SR 16
to SR 3. Take the exit for
Bainbridge Island and follow
signs for SR 305 north. Turn
left on SR 307 at the sign for
Hansville. Turn right on Point
No Point Road and park in the
dirt lot at the end of the road.
It's a short walk to the lighthouse.

The first lighthouse established on Puget Sound began service during a frigid week in January 1880 at the place where Admiralty Inlet pours into Puget Sound. The point was named by Captain Charles Wilkes during his 1841 expedition to map the waters of the area. As his ship approached the point it looked imposing, but on arrival he realized it was only a small spit of driftwood-strewn sand—no point at all.

The first keeper, a dentist from Seattle, hung a simple oil lamp in the lantern for a few days after his arrival until the lens was delivered and installed. The fifth order optic was mounted in a short brick tower. A fogbell that had formerly served at New Dungeness Light Station provided warnings in poor visibility. A duplex dwelling was situated about 250 feet south of the lighthouse.

In 1900, a fog signal building was attached to the tower to hold machinery for the operation of a kerosene-fueled fog trumpet. An oil house was built to hold the incendiary fuel. A few years later the lens was upgraded

to a fourth-order optic. Lightning struck the lighthouse in the 1920s and shook the lantern so hard it cracked the lens.

The station was automated in the 1980s. In 1997 the lighthouse was leased to Kitsap County Parks, which rented the keeper's quarters as a private residence. In 2008 the U.S. Lighthouse Society moved its headquarters into the south side of the duplex and converted the north side into a cozy vacation rental. Later that year the Coast Guard turned off the fog signal and relocated the light to a modern beacon on the lantern railing. The society hopes to relight the lens as a private beacon.

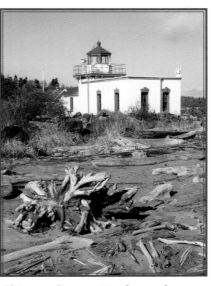

A broad driftwood-strewn beach wraps around Point No Point Lighthouse, where fishing is good off the point. Ships make a critical turn here as they enter or leave Puget Sound.

DIRECTIONS

See Point No Point Light for directions to Hansville. Entering the small community, pass Lighthouse Road on the right and continue about a tenth of mile where the road curves left and becomes Twin Spits Road. Drive another mile, and look for the Coast Guard sign on the right at a driveway. The lighthouse can be seen through the trees.

Built in 1965 by former Coast Guard lightkeeper and maritime author James Gibbs, the private lighthouse stands on the northern tip of the Kitsap Peninsula facing Admiralty Inlet. Gibbs was given the iron lantern from the defunct 1858 Smith Island Lighthouse and installed it on a wood frame tower adjoining his summer cottage. The beacon, which shows a fixed light, is an official aid to navigation. It is currently owned by a group who use it as a timeshare. It is not open to the public but can be seen from the road and from the water.

Former Tillamook Rock Lighthouse keeper and popular maritime historian, James Gibbs, built Skunk Bay Lighthouse in 1965 as a vacation cottage (above). The lantern room was taken from the defunct 1857 Smith Island Lighthouse (below), an Admiralty Inlet sentinel destroyed by erosion and abandoned by the 1960s. Over the years, Gibbs and other owners of Skunk Bay Light have added to the structure, seen from the back in 2006 on the opposite page.

Mukilteo Light Station   47.948N, 122.306W

FOR INFORMATION ON TOURS
Mukilteo Historical Society
304 Lincoln Avenue
Mukilteo, WA 98275
425.513.9602
www.mukilteohistorical.org

HOURS OF OPERATION
The station is open for tours
from April through Labor Day
on weekends from 12:00 P.M.
to 4:00 P.M. Consult the website or call for holiday hours
in December.

DIRECTIONS
From I-5, take the Mukilteo
Expressway exit 189 into
Mukilteo. Turn left at the ferry
dock and drive a half-block to
the lighthouse.

Occupied as a winter camp by native tribes for centuries before pioneer settlement, Mukilteo means "good camping ground" in Salish. Despite sawmills and shipbuilding in the area and considerable vessel traffic in Possession Sound, including ferries, a lighthouse was not built at Mukilteo until 1906. The new sentinel stood on Elliot Point at a critical turning place for ships ply- ing Possession Sound. The growing port at nearby Ev- erett was the final impetus for the construction of the lighthouse.

The $27,000 station con- sisted of a small wooden light tower and attached fog signal building. The tower was 38 feet tall and exhib- ited a fourth-order flashing Fresnel lens made by Sautter & Cie of Paris. Machinery for a fog trumpet was located on the ground floor. Two handsome keeper's dwellings flanked the lighthouse, while a windmill provided water for the homes and fog signal (top photo opposite page).

The station was electrified in 1927 when the lens was changed to a fixed fourth-order. It was automated in 1990, and the last keeper locked the doors. Shortly afterwards, the station was given to the city of Mukilteo and opened for tours. It has undergone consider- able restoration. There is a large gift shop in one of the old dwell- ings; exhibits occupy some of the buildings. Every September the Mukilteo Lighthouse Festival draws thousands of visitors.

During the December holiday season the lighthouse is decorated with lights (below).

Mulkiteo Centennial decorations

Point Wilson Light Station   48.144N, 122.75W

HOURS OF OPERATION
The lighthouse is open for tours on Sundays from mid-May through Labor Day. The surrounding park grounds are open year-round during daylight hours.

DIRECTIONS
From Main Street in Port Townsend, follow signs for Fort Worden State Park and the lighthouse.

The dangerous turn into Admiralty Inlet at Port Townsend was first marked in 1865 by a bell, which rang from a church in the port on foggy days and inspired the hymn "The Harbor Bell." There also was a lantern hung on a post at Point Hudson. A lens-lantern was placed on a small brick building on the point by 1900 (below). A better warning system came in 1879 when a lighthouse was built on Point Wilson, which jutted into the Strait of Juan de Fuca at its confluence with Admiralty Inlet. The point, part of Quimper Peninsula, was named for a member of Captain George Vancouver's crew during his 1792 exploration of the area.

The wooden lighthouse exhibited a fixed fourth-order Fresnel lens. The square tower rose from the roof of the keeper's dwelling. The station also included a fog whistle. Ruby panels were installed on the lens in 1894 to differentiate the beacon from nearby lights. By this time Fort Worden had been built on the bluff behind the light station as part of the triangle of defense established in the 1890s to protect Puget Sound. Its sister forts built at Fort Casey and Fort Flagler also had lighthouses.

A new 46-foot lighthouse and attached fog signal building was built in 1914. The old dwelling continued in use, but with its light tower gone. Coast Guard bungalows were added in the 1950s. The station was automated in 1976, and Coast Guard personnel continued to live in the dwellings until 2000.

Heavy storms continually chisel away the shoreline in front of the lighthouse. A new stone barrier was completed in 2005 but a storm the next year damaged it, and sand and rocks were thrown against the lighthouse. Repairs have temporarily rectified the problem but engineers believe the tower may have to be relocated in the future to save it. In 2008 the lens was discontinued, and a modern beacon was placed on the lantern railing. The foghorn also was discontinued.

The lighthouse is part of Fort Worden State Park and is located near a camping area. The local Coast Guard Auxiliary opens the tower for tours in summer.

Admiralty Head Lighthouse   48.16N, 122.68W

FOR MORE INFORMATION
Keepers of Admiralty Head
Lighthouse
P.O. Box 5000
Coupeville, WA 98239
360.679.7391
www.admiraltyhead.wsu.edu

HOURS OF OPERATION
Tour hours vary throughout the
year. Check the website or call
360.240.5584

DIRECTIONS
On Whidbey Island's Fort
Casey Road, a half mile north
of the Keystone Ferry Dock,
proceed into Fort Casey Park.
Follow signs for the lighthouse.

Built in 1861 on the southwest shore of Whidbey Island, the lighthouse was originally called Red Bluff Light. It was a wooden house with a lantern rising from its roof that displayed a fourth-order Fresnel lens (below). It served until Fort Casey was established on the point during the Spanish-American War. Army buildings upstaged the light, so it was moved back from the bluff and used as quarters.

Meanwhile, a new lighthouse was built in 1903 north of the bluff. The name was changed to Admiralty Head Lighthouse, in honor of the moniker bestowed on the point by Captain George Vancouver in 1792. The handsome Spanish-style design featured a spacious two-story residence attached to a cylindrical brick tower. A covering of parge gave the lighthouse its bright white daymark. Behind the lighthouse was a mule barn. The sentinel served until 1922 when it was discontinued because of changes in the shipping lanes.

Five years later the lens and lantern were removed and transferred across Admiralty Inlet to New Dungeness Lighthouse. Fort Casey closed after World War II, and the grounds and lighthouse became state park property. The lighthouse later was restored with a new lantern and opened to the public. It is not an active aid to mariners, but Lighthouse Environmental Programs, an arm of Washington State University and the current occupant of the lighthouse, has replaced the lantern with a historically correct replica. They hope to eventually relight the tower.

The beautiful lighthouse at Admiralty Head was designed by Astoria architect Carl Leick, who was responsible for the plans for about thirty-five lighthouses in the Pacific Northwest. Admiralty Head is one of his most unique designs. After the lighthouse was discontinued in the 1920s, the lantern was removed and transferred to New Dungeness Lighthouse. The current Admiralty Head lantern was installed by Washington State Parks, but a new, historically correct lantern being built at a local shipyard will crown the tower in a few years.

New Dungeness Light Station   48.18N, 123.11W

FOR MORE INFORMATION
New Dungeness Light Station Association
P.O. Box 1283
Sequim, WA 98382
360.683.9166
scheduling@newdungeness-lighthouse.com
www.newdungenesslighthouse.com

HOURS OF OPERATION
Tours of the lighthouse and museum are available daily from 10:00 A.M. to 4:00 P.M.

DIRECTIONS
From U.S. 101 in Sequim, turn right on Kitchen Dick Road and follow signs for New Dungeness National Wildlife Refuge. Park at the refuge entrance and hike to the lighthouse. The hike is eleven miles roundtrip and is best accomplished at low tide. Water, picnic tables, and a restroom are available at the lighthouse.

Captain George Vancouver named New Dungeness for its resemblance to a place in Kent, England by the same name. Dungeness Spit is a five-mile-long finger of sand created by the Dungeness River as it pours down from the Olympic Mountains into the Strait of Juan de Fuca. The spit encloses Sequim Bay.

The tip of the spit was marked with a 97-foot-tall lighthouse in 1857, the second oldest sentinel in Washington. The tower rose from a Cape Cod-style dwelling and exhibited a third-order Fresnel lens. A fogbell guided ships in periods of low visibility. The bell proved ineffective and was later replaced by a steam signal.

Life on the spit was challenging. The first keeper, Henry Blake, walked eleven miles roundtrip to court a young woman who lived in the settlement at New Dungeness. They eventually married, had children, and began the light station's long tenure as a family station.

The point was ideal for keeping livestock, fishing, and hunting the spit's many birds. The climate, referred to as the "Washington Banana Belt," was usually pleasant, even in winter. Occasional storms rattled the station, however, and heavy fogs formed on the cold deep waters of the Strait of Juan de Fuca.

With the addition of a steam fog signal in 1878 more work was required. Two more keepers were hired, bringing the total to four. Even so, it was sixteen years until a second dwelling was built. In the interim, keepers' families lived ashore to ease crowding at the station and to allow the children to attend school.

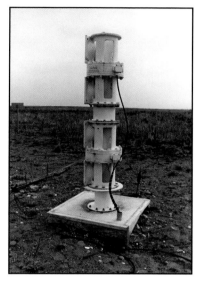

Earthquake and water damage took a toll on the tall lighthouse. In 1927, 30 feet of the upper brickwork on the tower were removed. The lantern from the defunct Admiralty Head Lighthouse was brought to the spit and installed on the shortened lighthouse, along with a fourth-order flashing lens.

The station was automated in 1994 with a modern optic and fog signal, and the lens was moved to the Coast Guard Museum Northwest in Seattle. By this time the entire spit was a wildlife refuge where vehicular traffic was forbidden. A local nonprofit group began staffing the light station 365 days a year. They were permitted to transport volunteer caretakers to the lighthouse in four-wheel vehicles. The New Dungeness Light Station "Keeper Program" was one of the first in the nation.

The New Dungeness Light Station Association continues to maintain the site. Members serve one-week stints as keepers. Their hard work has saved the light station from vandalism, deterioration, and possible loss. The group has also done restoration and established a small museum in the base of the lighthouse. Daily tours are offered, along with a rest area for hikers and picnickers.

New Dungeness Light has seen a progression of optics and fog signals in its long career. A bell was the first fog signal, then a steam horn. Electric foghorns were used after World War II (opposite page). There is no fog signal today, a result of modern navigational equipment used by ships. The lighthouse too has seen change. The old postcard image shows the lighthouse prior to earthquake and water damage, which necessitated removal of its top portion. Today, it is a popular retreat for vacationers seeking solitude.

Cattle Point Lighthouse

A livestock area on the southern tip of San Juan Island in the nineteenth century gave Cattle Point its name. In 1888, a lens-lantern mounted on a pole was the first navigational aid for ships approaching the island. It had an eight-day reservoir for kerosene. A lamplighter who lived nearby tended the lantern once a week.

In the early 1920s a radiobeacon was installed near the pole light, and Navy personnel were assigned to the site. In addition to operating the radiobeacon, which had sister stations at New Dungeness Lighthouse and Smith Island Lighthouse, the sailors began tending the pole light. In 1935 a 34-foot lighthouse replaced the pole beacon. It had no dwelling, but Navy personnel took care of the beacon until their radio station closed just before World War II. Then a lamplighter was again hired.

During automation of the lighthouse in the 1960s, the top of the lighthouse was removed to allow an exposed beacon to be installed. In the 1990s a faux lantern was placed back on the top of the lighthouse for a movie production, but it has since been removed. Today the lighthouse is part of the Department of Natural Resources and sits in Cattle Point Interpretive Area.

DIRECTIONS
The lighthouse is not open but the grounds are accessible. From Friday Harbor, take Cattle Point Road through San Juan Island Historic Site to Cattle Point Interpretive Area. A short grassy trail leads from the parking area to the lighthouse.

Lens-Lanterns

In the budget-tight era following the Civil War, the government cut corners on measures designed to mark the perils of the West Coast. One cost-saving device was the lens-lantern, a glorified kerosene lamp that ran unattended for eight days. Point Robinson, Washington (page 146) had several lens-lanterns to guide shipping through the foggy passage between Seattle and Tacoma. The first beacon was mounted on a simple wooden tower in 1887 (top). The light was difficult to see, so a taller wooden scaffold tower went up in the early 1890s (bottom). Point Robinson Light continued to operate with a lens-lantern until 1915 when a traditional lighthouse was built that exhibited a fifth-order lens.

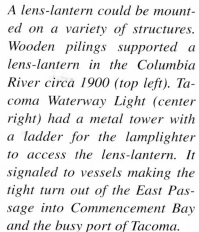

A lens-lantern could be mounted on a variety of structures. Wooden pilings supported a lens-lantern in the Columbia River circa 1900 (top left). Tacoma Waterway Light (center right) had a metal tower with a ladder for the lamplighter to access the lens-lantern. It signaled to vessels making the tight turn out of the East Passage into Commencement Bay and the busy port of Tacoma.

One of Washington's most peculiar lighthouses (bottom) marked Point Roberts, a small appendage of land south of Delta, British Columbia that was the result of a geopolitical dispute and subsequent treaty in 1846 establishing the western border between Canada and the United States at 49 degrees north latitude. The tiny thumb of land known as Point Roberts went to the Untied States. It was marked with a light shortly thereafter to guide shipping past shoals in Boundary Bay. The wooden lighthouse (shown left circa 1945) supported a lens-lantern. It was destroyed in a winter storm and was replaced by a metal skeleton tower with an electric beacon.

Burrows Island Lighthouse   48.477N, 122.71W

FOR INFORMATION ON BOAT
TOURS
NW Schooner Society
P.O. Box 9504
Seattle, WA 98109
800.555.NWSS
www.nwschooner.org

The small island facing Rosario Strait has had a lighthouse since 1906 to aid ships entering and leaving the labyrinth of waterways of the San Juan Islands. The integrated 34-foot wooden tower and fog signal building exhibited a fourth-order Fresnel lens with red sectors to warn of shoals to the south. A fog trumpet blared seaward from the west side of the sentinel. Steep cliffs around the site required construction of a boathouse with a derrick. A large, two-story dwelling for the keepers stood behind the lighthouse. Later, the Coast Guard added a bungalow.

Lightkeepers enjoyed an idyllic life on the little isle. Orcas swam by the station, and eagles nested in the trees. The small town of Anacortes was a short boat ride away. Yet there were dangers. Fenced yards and watchdogs helped ensure children did not wander off and fall into the water. Winter storms assailed the west-facing light station with heavy wind and rain, sometimes causing damage and preventing boat travel for long periods.

Boarded up, locked, and fenced to deter vandalism, quaint Burrows Island Light patiently awaits a steward to care for it. The fourth-order lens was removed in 1997 and placed in storage at the Coast Guard station in Port Angeles. A modern Vega beacon still signals to vessels in Rosario Strait.

The station was automated in 1972. The Fresnel lens was removed in 1997 in favor of a modern optic. The lighthouse has been transferred to the NW Schooner Society through the National Historic Lighthouse Preservation Act. The site is not open to the public, but the society hopes to conduct public tours in the future. Consult the website for information.

Lime Kiln Lighthouse   48.515N, 123.15W

FOR MORE INFORMATION
Friends of Lime Kiln Society
1567 Westside Road
Friday Harbor, WA 98250
www.folkssji.org

HOURS OF OPERATION
The lighthouse is open for
tours Memorial Day through
Labor Day on Thursday and
Saturday evenings from 7 P.M.
until sunset. The grounds are
open throughout the year during regular park hours from
sunrise to sunset.

DIRECTIONS
The lighthouse is located
in Lime Kiln State Park off
Westside Highway twelve
miles west of Friday Harbor.

**San Juan Island's dramat-
ic western shore** had lime
kilns in the 1860s. Nearby
a beacon was established in
1914 on a bluff overlooking
Dead Man's Bay. It guided
ships through Haro Strait,
a major portal to Vancou-
ver Island and the Georgia
Strait. The simple light was
a small drum lens on a pole
mounted on a square con-
crete box. It was maintained
by a local lamplighter.

In 1919 the site was up-
dated with a concrete light
tower and attached fog signal building. Two keepers'
homes were built on the
hill behind the lighthouse.
There was also a garage
and a cistern. The new lantern showed a fourth-order
flashing Fresnel lens that rotated in a mercury float. The light
was an incandescent oil vapor lamp until 1950 when electric
power finally reached the site. Stringing power lines to the remote station was expensive because of the distance to San Juan
Island from the power station at Anacortes and the necessity of
setting the power line poles into the extensive rock ledges on the
island's west side. Lime Kiln was the last lighthouse in Washington to be electrified.

Despite their cloistered existence, life at the station was idyllic for the keepers and their families. In summer the island was
dappled with wildflowers and orcas lounged in the lagoon below
the light tower. Sunsets and breath-taking scenery were perks.
Ships saluted the lighthouse as they passed. Later, cruise ships

moved silently past the sentinel on their way to the Georgia Strait and Alaska.

Automation came to the station in 1962. It then sat empty for twenty years. The 1980s saw much activity. In 1983 the lighthouse became a whale research facility operated by the Moclips Cetological Society. A year later the station became Lime Kiln State Park, and rangers took up residence in the old lightkeepers' dwellings. In

1987 the Coast Guard updated the lighthouse with a modern beacon visible 17 miles.

Today the lighthouse features a public whale-watching area and a small museum and gift shop. The research facility is managed by the Whale Museum of Friday Harbor. The tower is open for tours on select summer evenings.

Turn Point Light Station   48.688N, 123.237W

FOR MORE INFORMATION
Turn Point Lighthouse Preservation Society
P.O. Box 243
Orcas Island, WA 98280
info@tplps.org
www.tplps.org

DIRECTIONS
The lighthouse is closed at present, but the grounds are open as part of a state preserve. During the summer a resident docent is on hand daily to give tours. Stuart Island can be accessed by boat. Charters are available at Deer Harbor and Orcas Landing on Orcas Island, and at Friday Harbor on San Juan Island. Boats drop anchor at Prevost Harbor, then visitors walk a two-mile trail to the lighthouse.

Named for the point on Stuart Island where ships make an important turn between Boundary Pass and Haro Strait, the light began operation in 1893 as a lens-lantern mounted on a pole in front of a fog signal building housing a steam whistle. The light was visible about 7 miles. A spacious dwelling for two keepers sat on the hill behind the light. There was also a mule barn, oil house, cistern and water tower, and several work buildings.

Families enjoyed a quiet and sometimes lonely life at the station. There were few neighbors, and a one-room schoolhouse served the entire island. Two or three keepers were assigned to the lighthouse and fog signal. They also kept an eye out for rumrunners during Prohibition, since the light station was situated very near the Canadian border. Illegal liquor was easily smuggled from British Columbia through the San Juan Islands into mainland Washington.

A boat was supplied by the Lighthouse Service but it was a long trip to Friday Harbor or Bellingham. The families depended largely on the lighthouse tender to deliver supplies. During the 1930s when Edward Albee and Jens Pedersen served at Turn Point, there were nine children at the lighthouse, plus a dog, several cats, and a pet raccoon. The families also had a cow.

In the 1930s the beacon was upgraded and moved to a 16-foot concrete tower in front of the fog signal building, 44 feet above water. The station also was improved with a new electric horn. Since there was no electricity on the island, a generator was installed to run the horn. The station was automated in 1974 with a modern electric beacon and solarized a few years later. After 9-11, the Coast Guard installed surveillance equipment on top of the lighthouse to watch the Canadian border.

The property has been transferred to the Bureau of Land Management, which is working with the nonprofit Turn Point Lighthouse Preservation Society to restore the buildings and open the site to the public. A small museum is housed in the historic mule barn. The society offers at least one open house every summer.

Patos Island Lighthouse   48.789N, 122.97W

FOR MORE INFORMATION
Keepers of Patos Light
P.O. Box 518
Lopez Island, WA 98261
patoslightkeepers@hotmail.com
www.patoslightkeepers.org

DIRECTIONS
The lighthouse is accessible only by boat. Charters are available from Orcas Landing and Deer Harbor on Orcas Island and Friday Harbor on San Juan Island.

Located in the San Juan Islands on the western tip of Patos Island, the lighthouse was initially built in 1893 as a fog signal station to guide shipping through Boundary Pass, the portal between Haro Strait and the Strait of Georgia. A minor light on a pole served as the beacon. A large Victorian dwelling was situated in a wooded area behind the light. The name Patos, meaning "ducks," was bestowed by Spanish explorers in 1792.

In 1908 the pole light was removed, and a light tower was added to the fog signal building. The 38-foot lighthouse had a fourth-order lens with a range of 15 miles. With the Canadian border only about a mile away, it had international

coverage. A second dwelling was built for the assistant keeper. The station also had tanks for water storage, a barn, and a boathouse.

Life for the remote station's families was bittersweet. Helene Glidden, daughter of 1905 lightkeeper Edward Durgan, revealed the joys and hardships of her sequestered childhood in *A Light on the Island*. She wrote of Christmas gifts hidden in the oil house, of games in the tidepools and woods, and rumrunners hiding out on the island, but also of the 25-mile boat trip to Bellingham for groceries and to fetch a doctor. One year, several of the thirteen Durgan children came down with smallpox. The keeper flew the flag upside-down as a call for help, but it was days until a doctor arrived.

In 1958 the old dwellings and other buildings were torn down and replaced with Coast Guard housing. The station was automated in 1974. The lens was replaced by a modern beacon a few years later. The Bureau of Land Management took over the site in the late 1990s and is restoring the buildings with the help of the nonprofit Keepers of Patos Light. The island is a state park with primitive camping facilities. The lighthouse is open for tours on select days in summer.

Saving the Sentinels

Saving America's treasured lighthouses has been largely a grassroots effort. The U.S. Lighthouse Society, the first nonprofit group to seek preservation of all lighthouses in the nation, was founded in 1985 in San Francisco by former Coast Guard officer Wayne Wheeler. It made its mark almost immediately with the creative conversion of several lighthouses into museums, hostels, and bed and breakfast inns. For the first twenty-three years of its existence the society operated from an office building in San Francisco's financial district. In 2008 it relocated to the Point No Point Lighthouse in Hansville, Washington. It continues to serve the preservation and education needs of the nation's lighthouses from this historic site overlooking the confluence of the Strait of Juan de Fuca and Puget Sound.

The U.S. Lighthouse Society is headquartered in the 1879 keepers' dwelling at Point No Point Lighthouse, with a million-dollar view over the confluence of the Strait of Juan de Fuca and Puget Sound. Note the old U.S. Lighthouse Establishment flag flying beneath "Old Glory." The society is the oldest national organization devoted to the preservation of the nation's lighthouses.

For More Information

DeWire, Elinor. *Guardians of the Lights: Stories of U.S. Lighthouse Keepers*. Sarasota, FL: Pineapple Press, 1995.

DeWire, Elinor. *The Field Guide to Lighthouses of the Pacific Coast*. St. Paul, MN: Voyageur Press, 2006.

Gibbs, James. *Lighthouses of the Pacific*. West Chester, PA: Schiffer Publishing, 1986.

Leffingwell, Randy, and Pamela Welty. *Lighthouses of the Pacific Coast*. Stillwater, MN: Voyageur Press, 2000.

Nelson, Sharlene, and ted Nelson. *California Lighthouses*. San Luis Obispo, CA: E-Z Nature Books, 2006.

Nobel, Dennis. *Lighthouses and Keepers*. Annapolis, MD: Naval Institute Press, 1997.

Roberts, Bruce, and Ray Jones. *Pacific Northwest Lighthouses*. Old Saybrook, CT: Globe Pequot Press, 1997.

Shanks, Ralph, and Lisa Woo Shanks. *Guardians of the Golden Gate: Lighthouses & Lifeboat Stations of San Francisco Bay*. Petaluma, CA: Costaño Books, 1990.

Online Sources

American Lighthouse Foundation
P.O. Box 565, Rockland, ME 04841
207.594.4174
info@lighthousefoundation.org
www.lighthousefoundation.org

U.S. Lighthouse Society
9005 Point No Point Rd. NE, Hansville, WA 98340
415.362.7255
info@uslhs.org
www.uslhs.org

Lighthouse Friends
www.lighthousefriends.com

Index

About the Author

Elinor DeWire has been researching, photographing, and writing about lighthouses since 1972. She has visited more than eight hundred sentinels in the United States, Canada, the Caribbean, Europe, and Australia and is the author of sixteen books and more than 150 articles on the subject.

Former Coast Guard historian, Dr. Robert Scheina, calls her "America's most prolific lighthouse author and a driving force behind the recent upsurge in interest in preserving lighthouses and the history and nostalgia surrounding them." DeWire has been honored for her work by the U.S. Lighthouse Society, the American Lighthouse Foundation, and the National League of American Pen Women. Two of her books have won the coveted Ben Franklin Award and the Coast Guard Book Award. She lives in the Puget Sound area of Washington and teaches at Olympic College. Her husband, Jonathan, a retired navy officer, and her two grown children, Jessica and Scott, have fond memories of the family's many travels to lighthouses.

Other Books by Elinor DeWire

Guide to Florida Lighthouses
Guardians of the Lights: Stories of U.S. Lighthouse Keepers
The Lightkeepers' Menagerie: Stories of Animals at Lighthouses
Lighthouses: Sentinels of the American Coast
Lighthouses of the Mid-Atlantic
Lighthouses of the South
Field Guide to the Lighthouses of the New England Coast
The Lighthouses of Greece
The Lighthouse Activity Book
Florida Lighthouses for Kids
The Florida Night
Activities for Young Astronomers
*The DeWire Guide to the Lighthouses of Alaska, Hawai'i and the
    U.S. Pacific Territories.*

184